PAGES FROM OUR HISTORY

BY THE PEOPLE OF FOVANT

Dr. R.C.C. Clay (1890–1971), the third generation of his family to be the resident doctor of Fovant, was also a noted local historian. Over the years he collected snippets of historical information from which he prepared a set of papers entitled 'Some Notes on the History of Fovant'.

In the Foreword to his original material he wrote,

'These notes are in no way intended to be a complete History of Fovant; but, rather, a number of bricks heaped together, to which a future historian, having dug deeply, may add bricks, and with mortar of his own set them together – his bricks and mine, and so reconstruct the fabric of the past'.

Gratefully acknowledging his sure foundation we have started the rebuilding process by adding some bricks of our own. We will not complete this structure however for history is a continuous process, and there will be many more 'bricks' awaiting the next generation of historical research builders.

Pages from our History

by the people of

FOVANT

First published in the United Kingdom in 2005 by
The Hobnob Press, PO Box 1838, East Knoyle, Salisbury SP3 6FA
in association with the Fovant History Interest Group

British Library Cataloguing in Publication Data
A catalogue record for this book is available from the British Library.

ISBN 0-946418-39-X

Typeset in 10/15 pt Lucida Bright
Typesetting and origination by John Chandler
Printed in Great Britain by Salisbury Printing Company Ltd, Salisbury

Contents

Foreword

AT THE INAUGURAL MEETING of the Fovant History Interest Group in July 2000 discussion centred on how to collate the findings of those people in the village who had an interest in various aspects of its history. This led to the conclusion that the prime need was to make an index of sources. With such a database readily available to any researcher, no one person would be faced with the somewhat onerous task of writing up a collective village history. It was agreed that the way forward was to set up a website. The first phase of that website, (www.fovanthistory.org) now in place, continues to acquire a wealth of source material, which will in due course be added to that already on site.

However, some people do not have access to a computer, or would prefer to have the written word in a book in their hands. It is for these people that we have produced this book. It cannot really be called the book of the website because the site is continually updated, while a book can only contain material we happen to have at the moment of its publication. Additionally, we have too much information for it all to be included in one book. Accordingly we have extracted material from those pages which we consider to be of most general interest to act as a basis for each of the chapters which the book contains.

As individual group members have made themselves responsible for the text of a subject of their choice, there is no one author for the book. Indeed, there is a multiplicity of authors, for while some members have written up their chosen chapter in its entirety, others have linked the writings of the many people who have contributed articles to our website. Appropriately, all the material has been written by people of Fovant, be they current residents, or those who have close connections with the village. Since that is the case, it is fair to say that we, the people of Fovant, are engaged in writing our own history.

Since history has no precise beginning or ending, the task of researching and recording our village history is endless. Much has been gleaned from the past, written up by many in the present, for those who are yet to come, but there is always more to discover.

What can you add?

J.O.H. - 2005

Acknowledgements

MANY PEOPLE helped in the writing of this book. In the first instance members of the Fovant History Interest Group each contributed the chapter of their own individual interest. By each of their names in the list below their initials, which will appear at the end of their chosen chapter in the book, are appended in brackets.

Additionally, many of the sources used in the preparation of this book reflect the voices of villagers of Fovant, and nearby communities, who can remember events of their youth or stories that they have been told by previous generations.

Accordingly, grateful thanks are due to all of the following people with the hope that we haven't left anyone out.

Bernard Allnutt
Harry Ames - Naishes Farm
Jim Attfield - Dorchester Society of Friends
Betty and John Bacon
Ann Barnard (née Lee)
Wally Barrow
Mollie Baxter
Jenny Berwyn-Jones
Betty and Rob Boatwright
Joan and Roy Brooks
Brian Burton
Elsie Burton
Jenny Cater
Bunty Caverhill
Dorothy Clay
Tracy Combes
Jean Coombes
Tom Coombes
Nick Cowen
Diane Crockett
Keith Davies
John Eade
Pam Fenton
Barry Gallear
David Greenwood
Liz Harden (J.O.H.)
Mike Harden (M.C.L.H.)
Fred Harman
Ann Harris
Betty Harte (née Austin)
Valerie Heale
M Holley
Edgar Jay
Sue Jay
Tim Jefferson
Mary Jefferson (née Kirman - M.K.K.)

Stephen Jeffery
Willie Langdon
Mary and Bryan Lee
Barry Luffman
Margaret Mackenzie (M.A.M.)
Fiona and Tim Marshall
Sue Martindale (S.M.)
Nicky and Adrian Matthews (A.M.)
Gordon Morse
Olive Mullins
John Newman - Compton Farm
Freda Norris
Ali and Andy Nuttall
Audrey Nuttall
Roy Nuttall
Beryl Paton (B.P.)
Tony Pinder
Adrian Price
Jane Pybus
Don Shaw
Roy Simper
Judy Snowdon
Christine Thompson
Ian Townsend
Frank Turner
John Turner
Ken Walker
Val and Tony Wells
Grace Wray (née Cowdry)
Marjorie and Sid Wyatt
Peter Wyatt

With the obvious exception of Nick Cowen's sketches of flints on page 26, all artwork is by Liz Harden. Photographs appearing in the book mainly come from the F.H.I.G. photograph collection. Others have been loaned by some of the people acknowledged above or are from sources listed previously.

Finally, we must express our thanks to the Local Heritage Initiative who, through a partnership scheme involving the Heritage Lottery Fund, the Nationwide Building Society and the Countryside Agency, funded the publication of the book.

1
Historical Overview

LIKE MANY OTHER small, enclosed, rural communities, the village of Fovant was relatively bypassed by the larger historical events of national concern. However, the village was not entirely cut off from outside influence, so it is worth noting any village contact with such events within the context of our own parochial history.

Fovant is so hidden from view that you would be hard pressed to know that it is there. It is not only invisible from the top of our Downs, but even a traveller passing along the A30 road would hardly notice it. The village itself, nestling in its own little valley at right angles to the major road, sits on an interesting array of different types of rock. Water is plentiful, as witnessed by springs, a brook and several man-made lakes. Man has also imposed his mark on the village in the shape of the various boundaries, enclosures, roads and footpaths which either surround, or run through, the village. Documentation of the geography of the village ranges from the Anglo Saxon Charters, through a proliferation of 18th and 19th century mapmakers up to the present day.

There is some indication of Early and Middle Bronze Age settlement on Fir Hill and Chiselbury. Evidence of Roman influence in the area is also indicated by the discovery of a Romano-British bust in Sutton Mandeville and some small finds connected with the three stone cist burials, found on the hill above the north end of Dinton Road. Broadly speaking though, the village was scarcely inhabited until the Early Middle Ages when the Saxons invaded Britain. The Saxon Land Charters of AD 901 and AD 904, each mention *Fobbefunta*, the Saxon name for Fovant.

By the tenth century most of the country had the essential framework of central and local government already in place in which, for administrative purposes, the country was divided into counties and then subdivided into Hundreds. Each Hundred, an area thought to contain one hundred dwellings, had its own county court, and its sheriff and his officials ran the county, or shire as it was more generally known at the time. After their conquest of the country the Normans continued to use this efficient system in order to impose their own rule on the country. Undoubtedly this governmental structure would also have proved its worth during the production of the Domesday Book in which the conquerors listed all the country's goods and chattels.

Fovant is still nominally in the Hundred of Cawden and Cadworth and has a small entry in the Domesday Book

During this period Fovant's original church, thought to have been sited over an earlier Saxon place of worship, was built. No date is known for this church, but its first incumbent, Rob. de Hulcott, was listed as being in office in 1305. By the 15th century this church needed rebuilding and it was at this time that the church tower was added.

At the dissolution of the monasteries in the 16th century, the Abbess of Wilton, dispossessed of Wilton Abbey, was granted lands, a pension and a house in Fovant for herself and some of her nuns. Wilton Abbey, its lands and wealth, were then given to William Herbert, who later became the 1st Earl of Pembroke. As Fovant was one of the villages which came within this 'gift', William Herbert became its feudal lord, with all that the title entails. This situation remained largely unchanged until the sale of Pembroke lands in August 1919.

Religious dissent had a further impact on Fovant during the latter part of the 17th century, when a group of Quakers became active in the village. By the end of the 18th century they had moved away. They were followed in the early 19th century by a religious group calling themselves 'Dissenters'.

By this time the Lower Road, currently the A30, had been turnpiked, superseding that which went over the Downs as the major road to the West. Carriers, passenger and mail coaches plied to and fro between local towns and villages. Employment opportunities were expanded and were further enhanced by the mid 19th century opening of the Salisbury and Yeovil Railway, with its station at nearby Dinton. Although people could now move into and out of the village for a host of different purposes, statistically the population remained relatively constant until the mid 20th century.

Self-help in the form of various provident societies had always played a large part in village life. Fovant was also fortunate in having had a resident medical man since the late 18th century. Our school was opened in 1847, well before the Education Act of 1870 required the provision of educational facilities for all children. A village constable was noted as resident in the 1841 census, a sub-postmaster is listed in Kelly's Directory of 1855 and our Parish Council was set up in 1896.

During the Great War of 1914–18 Fovant, along with nearby villages, became the site for a very large military camp. Built at the foot of our Downs, an endless array of huts housed large numbers of soldiers. These men, though mainly in transit, still found time to carve their regimental badges on the Downs. The effect of their presence on the village was immense and lasting. The 1939–45 war largely bypassed the village in the military sense. However, we did have our own Home Guard unit, there was a searchlight battery in a field beside the Poplar Inn, and at least one German aircraft crashed nearby. Fovant also hosted some unaccompanied evacuee children.

Our first social housing was built in the 1950s. Mains water was finally installed throughout the village by 1950. Electricity provision, started in 1931, was extended in the 1950s and completed its final phase in the early 1960s. A modern drainage system also relieved the village in the early 1960s. With all services now in place, many new houses were built. The stage was then reached whereby no further development outside the existing village framework was possible due to the landscape constraints imposed. Consequently a lot of 'infilling' took place. Obviously an expansion of the population followed. Even so, the current population stands at well below the thousand mark.

The newcomers, blending into existing groups and organisations, brought a breath of outside air into the village. Invariably they joined in with the activities that constituted the social life of the village, and, in some cases, introduced new ideas which gave rise to the formation of new interest groups. We have a host of such clubs, covering a wide range of interests and activities, some of which were represented in the temporary Fovant Millennium Group which organised the village's celebrations on entry into the 21st century.

Village social cohesion was aided over the years through shared experience, made possible through such inventions as that of the internal combustion engine, the telephone, the wireless, the television and the computer. The latest improvement in village communications, access to Broadband, a fast Internet service, brings those of us who wish it into instant contact with other people anywhere in the world. Fovant is no longer an 'enclosed' community.

This précis of our village's history during the last two thousand years merely introduces the subject material of the chapters which follow and they in themselves barely scrape the surface of the information we have on our web site. You can log on to www.fovanthistory.org or contact any of us for further information.

J.O.H.

2
Village Geography

FOVANT is a parish of some 890 hectares (2,200 acres), lying between Salisbury in Wiltshire and Shaftesbury in Dorset. It is ten miles from each, by the A30 road. Apart from a short period during World War I, it has been a rural community whose inhabitants largely derived their livelihood from agriculture.

The physical geography of the area has determined the position and scale of the village, together with its communications and appearance. The scenery is affected by what is beneath it and how this has changed over millions of years. Since the village was first settled, landowners have found it necessary to establish their boundaries and, controversially, their rights. As the means became available, maps were made, not only to show communication between communities, but also to describe their shape and surroundings. Communication within villages developed. Paths appeared, became tracks and roads and then often reverted to paths again. Their upkeep provided employment for some villagers.

Scenery and Geology

An appreciation of the varied scenery surrounding Fovant, from rolling downland to flat terraces and wooded slopes, can be gained by taking a walk from the top of the downs to the southeast of the village, where there was once a turnpike road, down the steep chalk slope and across the gently-rising terrace, where agriculture is prominent, before again walking down over the steep north-facing wooded slope towards the Nadder and its alluvial soils, water meadows and mills.

This scenery reflects the underlying geology, which is interesting, as the village straddles the boundary between rocks typical of the Vale of Wardour, such as Chilmark limestone, and those of the chalk countryside. Fovant owes the shape of its landscape to happenings of up to 20 million years ago, when movements in the earth's crust, as the continents collided, resulted in the uplift of the Alps. In England the ripples produced arch-like structures, or anticlines, connected by shallow troughs. The arches are characterised by steep northern limbs, the southern limbs having only a gentle inclination.

To the south, the underlying rock is most obviously Chalk, that landscape feature which is apparent from the Dorset Downs, across Salisbury Plain and to the Marlborough and Berkshire Downs and beyond. Chalk hill-figures, of which Fovant has more than its fair share, are common in this landscape. This material, over 1,600 feet thick, was laid down from marine deposits during the Cretaceous period, some 100 million years ago. Nearer to the village, however, the picture becomes more complicated as older rocks become exposed.

Fovant itself is in a north-south valley and a wide terrace of Greensand bounds it on both east and west. This terrace was ideal on which to site military camps during World War I, signs of which may still be seen. The green-tinged stone was obviously used to build many of the older cottages in the village and several overgrown quarries are still discernible. Greensand also dates from the Cretaceous period, although of a lagoon rather than a marine environment.

The brook running through the village, which rises in springs at West Farm, has eroded the Upper Greensand, exposing Gault, where the deposits

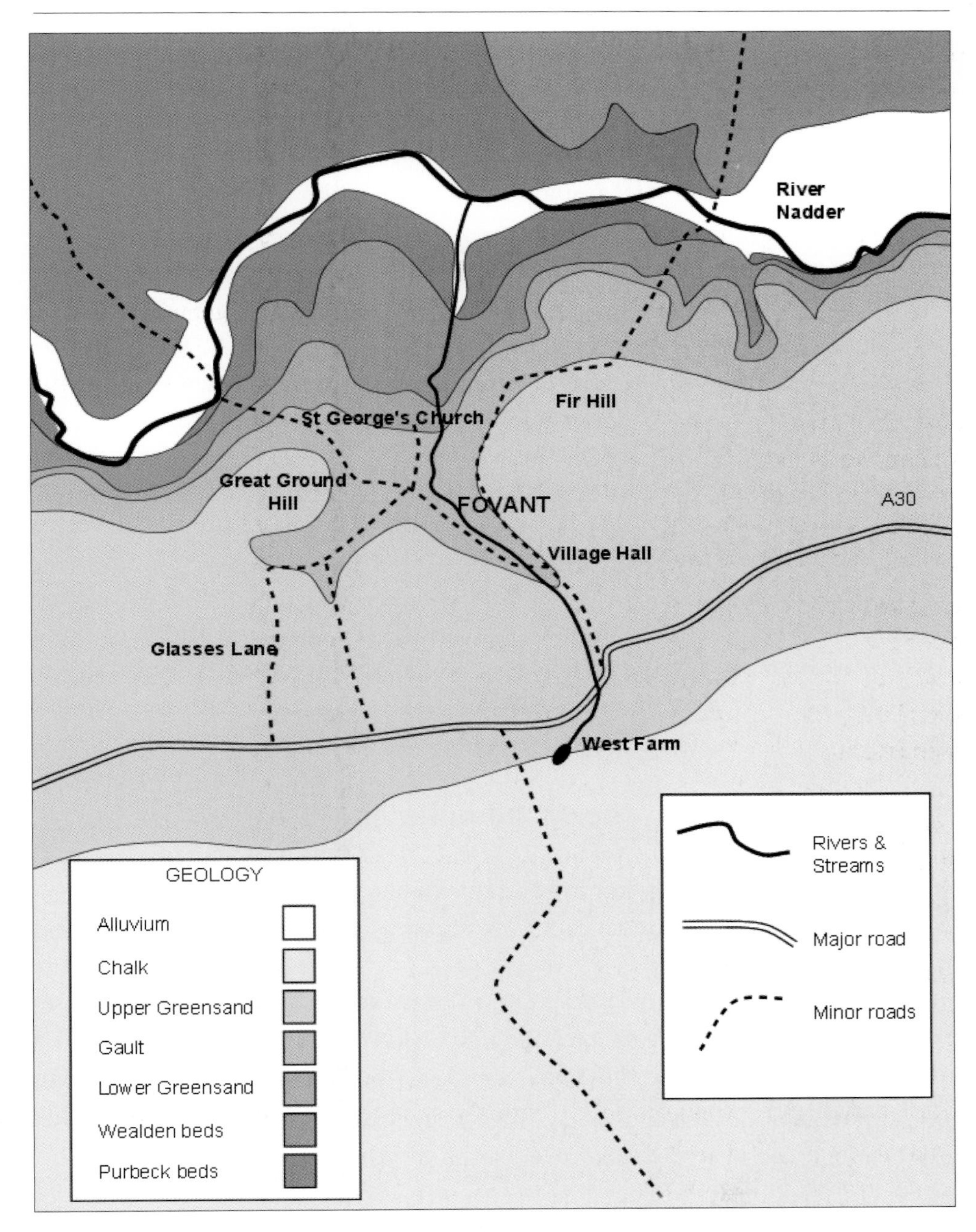

Geology of the area around Fovant

are mostly clays, and Lower Greensand, where sandy beds predominate. The Gault clays underlie most of the area from St George's Church and Glasses

Lane to the Village Hall and form the upper northern slopes of Fir Hill and Great Ground Hill, whilst Lower Greensand is a narrower strip, lower down on those slopes. The brook itself contains water that is pure enough for the cultivation of watercress and old records speak of water mills. It is now a popular fishing stream, accompanied by artificial shallow lakes and a fish farm.

The erosion continues in the valley of the River Nadder into which the stream flows, exposing other rock, the Wealden beds, or grey loam, which are the earliest deposits of the Cretaceous period and represent the boundary between that period and the fresh-water deposits laid down in the Jurassic period.

Deposits north of the village represent the most easterly exposures of the rocks known as the Purbeck beds. These limestones are common in the nearby Vale of Wardour, together with the older Chilmark stone. They were deposited some 170 million years ago.

The area was not covered by a sheet of ice during the Ice Age, but the changes occurring then in climate and sea level influenced the deepening and widening of river valleys. Evidence of Early man has been found in the Avon and Stour valleys, so it is likely that the Nadder valley contains similar evidence.

Saxon boundaries

COMMUNITIES have always needed to establish their borders. The Saxons indicated their boundaries by describing obvious landmarks in Land Charters.

Much of the work on Saxon Land Charters was carried out by Dr G.B. Grundy. In an article in the Archaeological Journal. Vol. LXXVI of 1919 he identified two surveys, the first dated AD 901. This stated that King Eadward granted the area of '10 hides' to the thegn *Wihtbrord* and of this he writes:

> The extant copy of the survey is certainly at least founded on an Anglo-Saxon original, and is probably itself of pre-Conquest date. Whether it is the record of the survey made at the time of the grant is open to doubt.

The boundaries were indicated by the identification of succeeding landmarks and many of these are still recognisable today, either as features or as surviving names. This may be seen when superimposing them on a modern map.

For example, both surveys refer to ***Cock's Spring*** at the head of a small valley that runs up from the Nadder to Fovant Wood. The name persists, although corrupted, in Woodcock Corner.

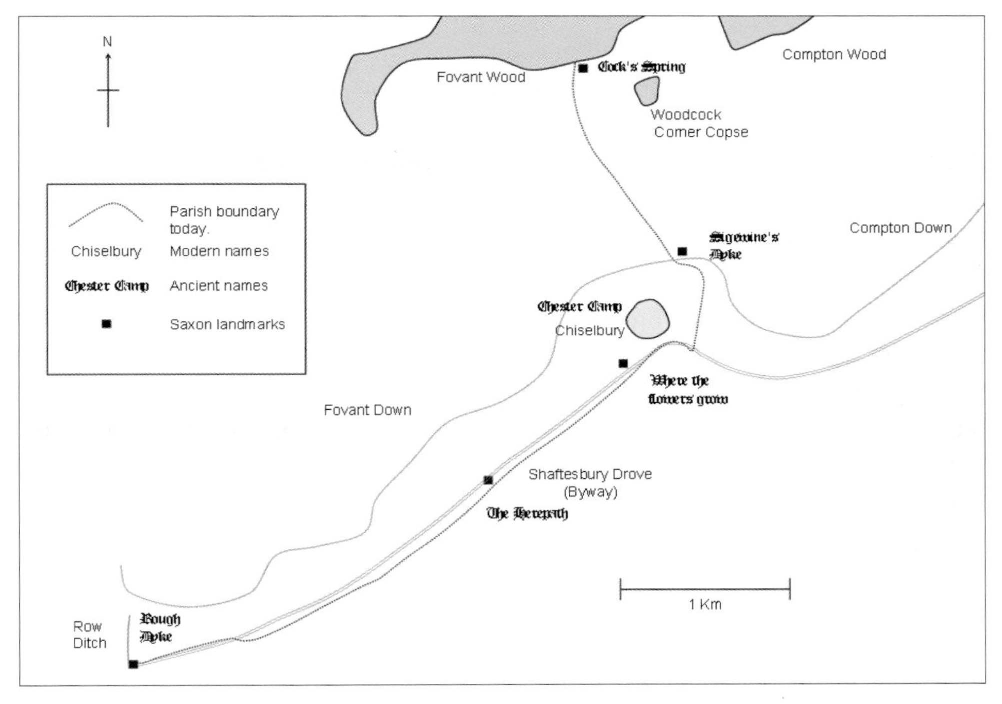

Fovant - ancient and modern

Dr Clay, in his examination of the Charters, thought that ***Sigewine's Dyke*** referred to a hollow-way that runs up the downs to sweep round the feature that we know as Chiselbury, which the survey identified as ***Chester Camp***. The next landmarks described were **thirty rods east of Chester Camp where the Flowers grow** and then **the Burial place**. Although Dr Clay's excavations in 1928 failed to find a burial place, he did record a patch of 'the very handsome and conspicuous Greater Willow Herb', remarking that 'it is pleasing to think that this same patch existed and flowered in Saxon days'.

One prominent boundary, ***The Herepath,*** survives as a byway, whilst part of the word itself survives as the German *heer* or army. It is therefore likely that the track was thought of as wide enough for an army to use.

In Sutton Mandeville, a boundary point named ***Rough Dyke*** survives today as Row Ditch.

A further charter, dated 994, granted by King Aethelred (978-1016), gave land to the church of St. Mary the Virgin at Wilton and later on, an extract from the Domesday Book, made in 1086, reads, *'The same church (Wilton) holds Fobefont'* (it lists ploughlands, meadows and mills, but not a church). The growth of the village in the next seven hundred years is an interest which our History Group intends to pursue.

The Enclosure Award of 1787

MUCH OF ENGLAND had been enclosed - that is, divided into separate fields - since medieval times, but in the eighteenth century enclosure by agreement began to give way to enclosure by act of Parliament. The enclosures in Fovant and the neighbouring villages were described in the Enclosure Award of 1787.

This Award not only defined the boundaries of the fields in the Parish, but also the roads, carriageways and bridle paths.

Parliament appointed surveyors to establish the enclosures and they first met at Fovant Hut on 19th September 1785. By the time of their thirteenth meeting at 'the House of Morris Coward, known by the sign of the Greyhound in Wilton', they were hearing objections from Fovant residents concerning roads and paths. Their decisions were published on the 7th August 1786 in the Salisbury & Winchester Journal. Some indication of the use of the land and the practices thereon were also considered in their deliberations. For example:

> Two acres of downland lying north of the old turnpike road were given to the parish of Fovant as a poor furze allotment in which the poor of the parish might gather furze (gorse) for firewood, together with a smaller plot at the foot of the downs.
>
> Grass growing on, or on the sides of, the private carriage roads, by, or in the common fields, belonged to the tenants of the land bordering these roads.
>
> Landshards or Boundaries were to be left between the several allotments.
>
> A ten-acre field lying south of Touching Head Copse was given to the Rev. Eyre in return for his assistance to the surveyor in framing the enclosure

awards (although this piece of land was afterwards exchanged for another, probably on Moor Hill).

The names of the enclosures can be seen on the following maps.

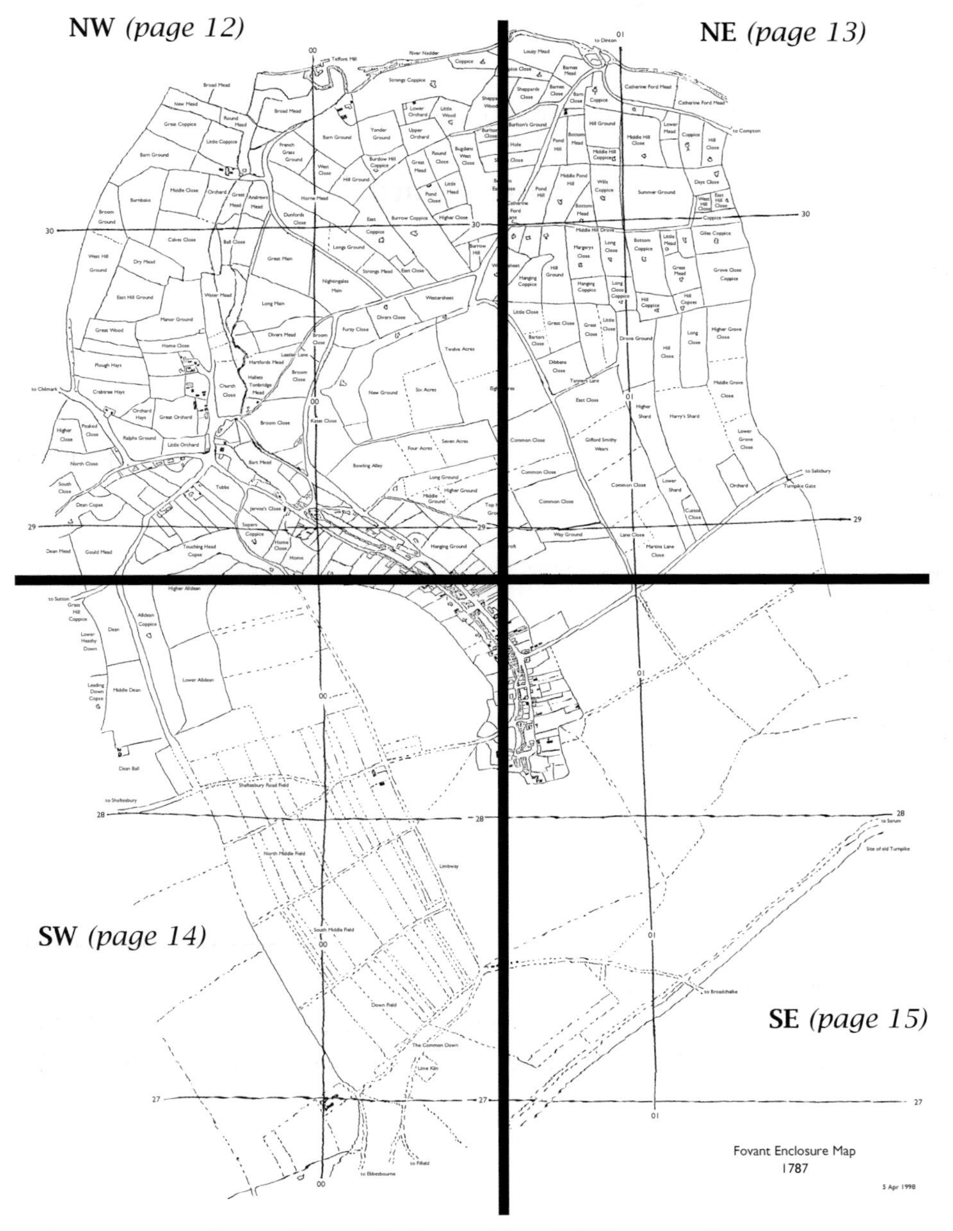

Key to Fovant Enclosure Map, 1786, transcripts

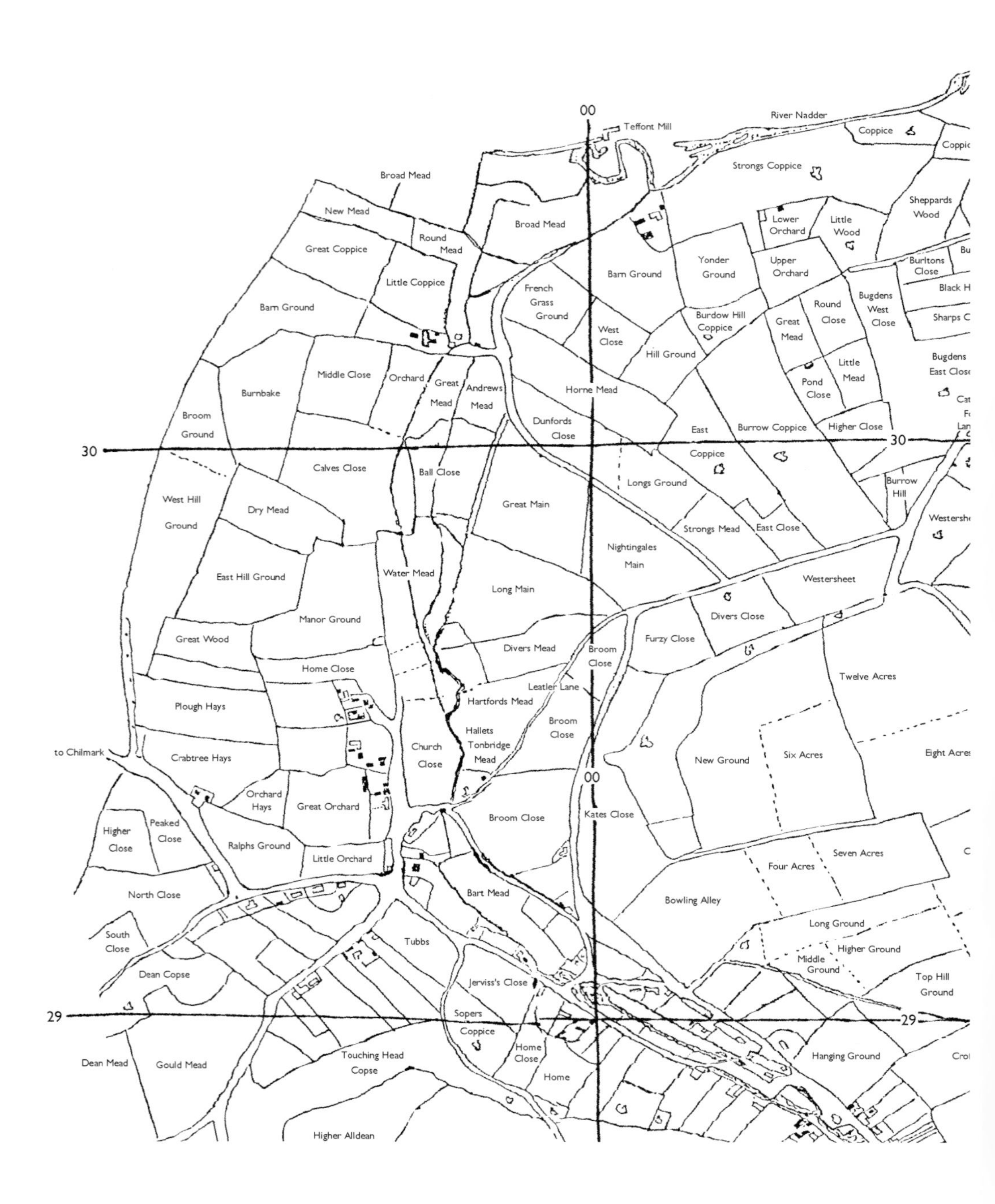

Fovant Enclosure Map, 1786, transcript, NW quadrant

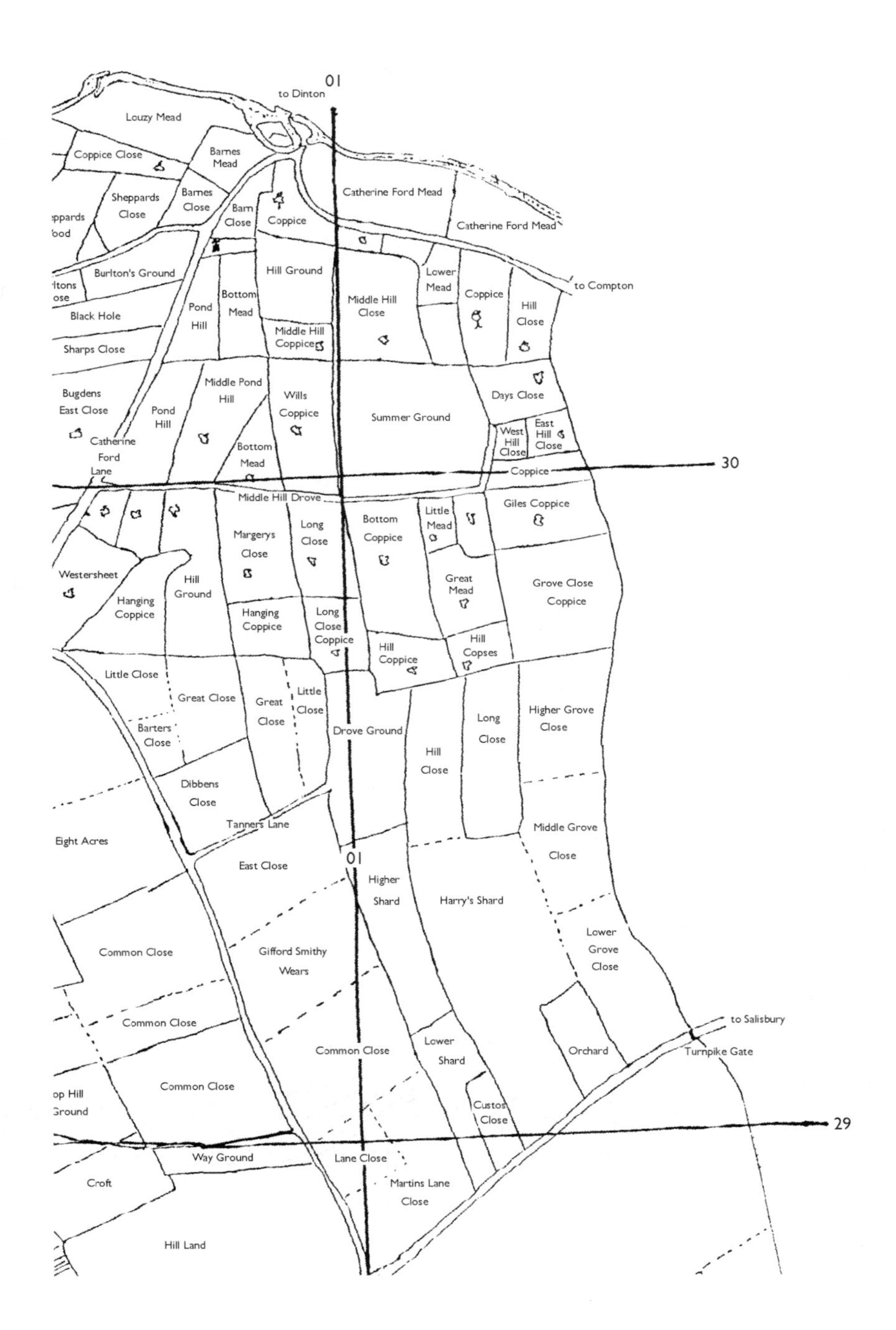

Fovant Enclosure Map, 1786, transcript, NE quadrant

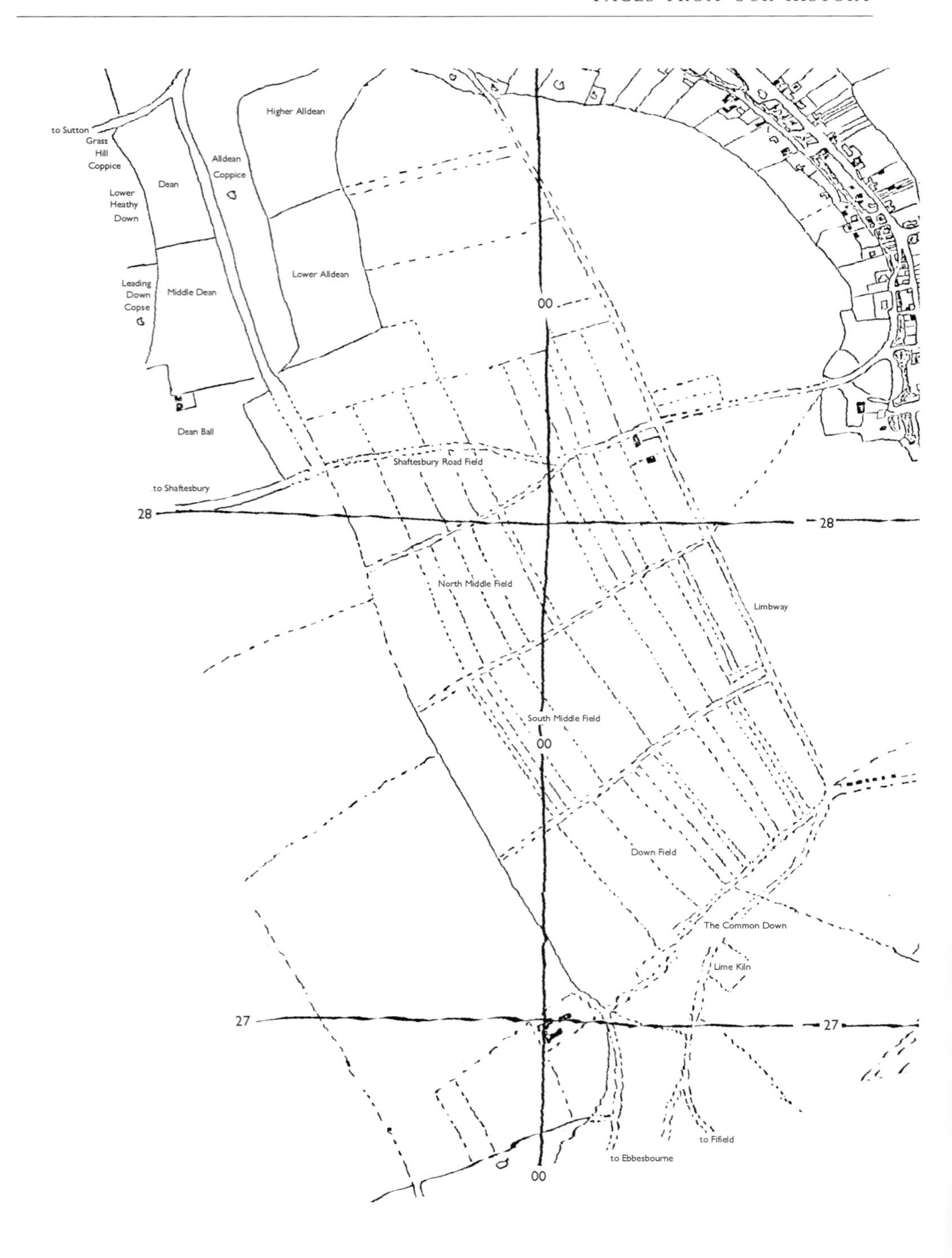

Fovant Enclosure Map, 1786, transcript, SW quadrant

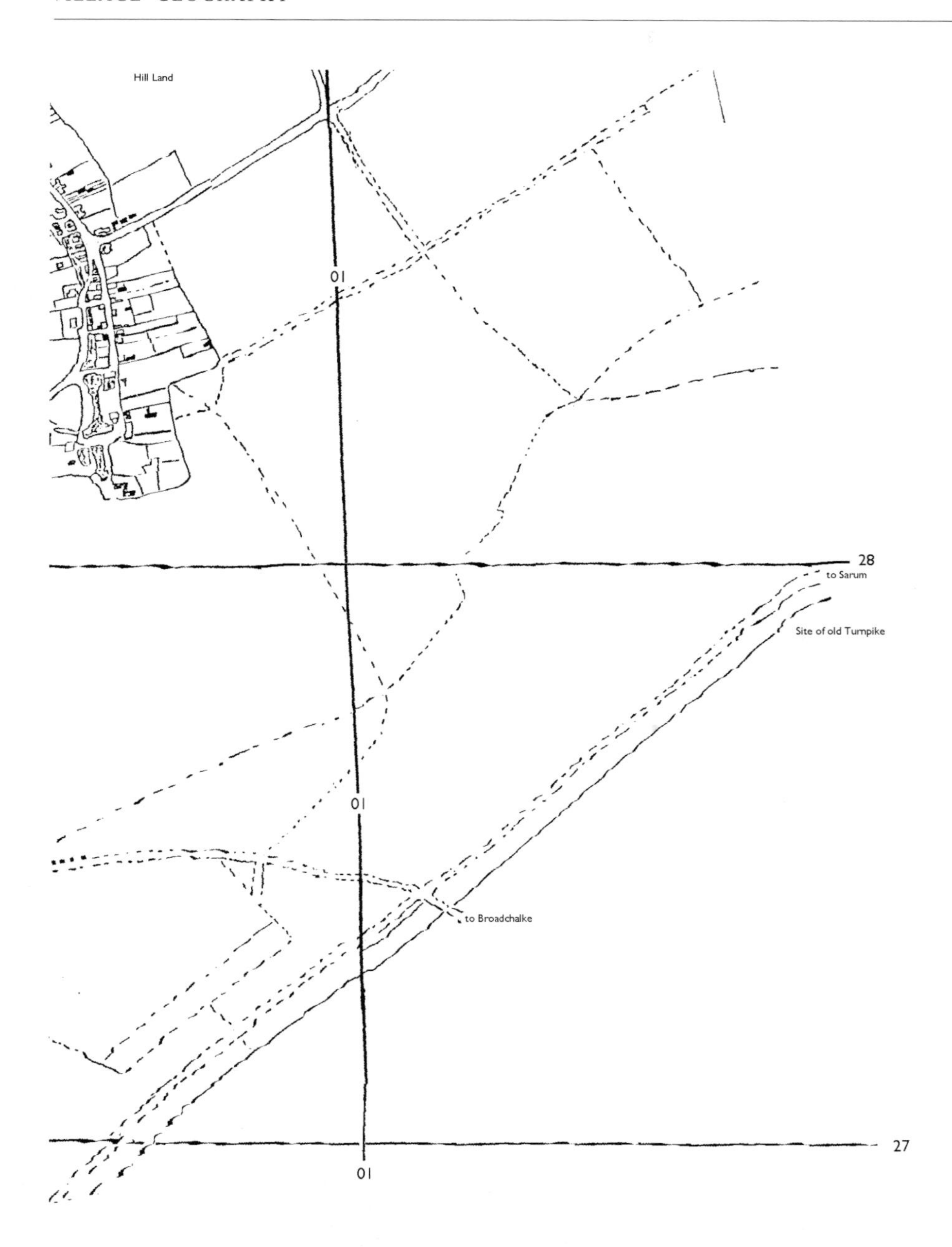

Fovant Enclosure Map, 1786, transcript, SE quadrant

Maps of Fovant

WHILST ROAD MAPS of the country had been produced in the sixteenth century, one of the first useful maps showing Fovant itself was that produced by John Andrews and Andrew Dury in 1773. This was in response to a prize offered by the Royal Society of Arts for county maps at a scale of one inch to one mile. By that time, the spelling of Fovant had become accepted, at least by map-makers, although since the oldest form of the village name that had been met with (in the Saxon Charters) was Fobbefunte, at least another thirty versions of the name had been used elsewhere.

A number of maps have been collected into a book *Printed Maps of Wiltshire 1787-1844*, published by the Wiltshire Record Society in 1996 and edited by Dr John Chandler. Extracts from some of these maps have been included here and are reproduced by permission.

The extracts may be compared with the map shown in the previous section, to see how (or indeed if) Fovant has changed through the centuries.

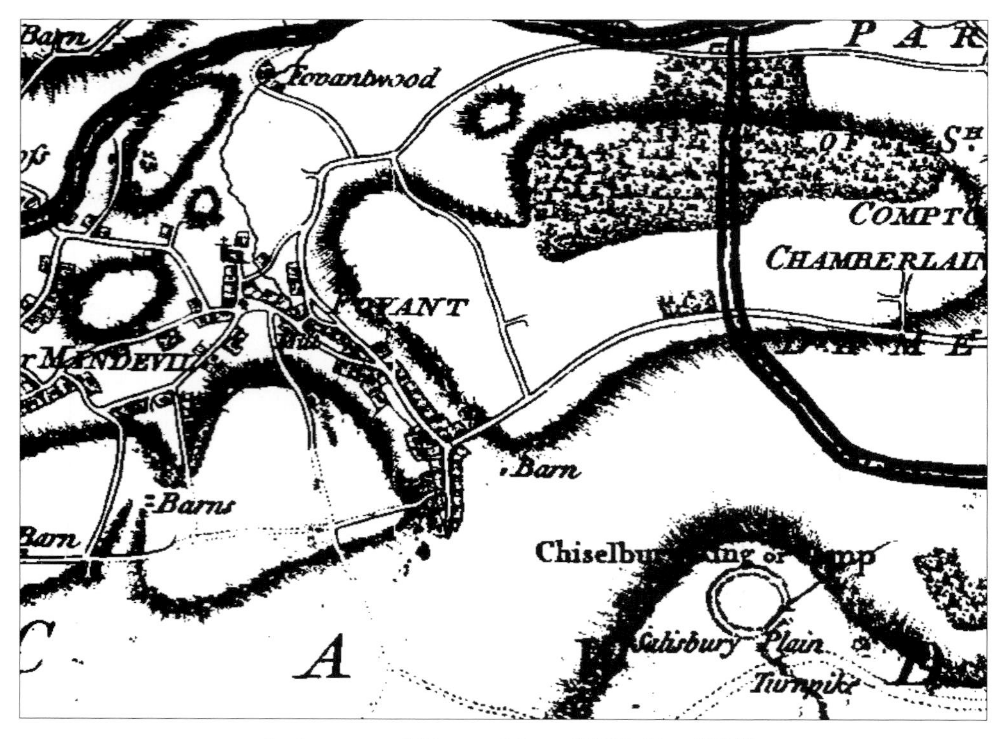

Andrews and Dury - Map of Wiltshire 1773

Comparison with a modern map shows the shape of the village and its roads to be very much as they are today. The woods near Fovant seem to be quite sparse, although towards Compton Chamberlayne they were shown to be extensive, as they still are.

Long before the use of contour lines, there was some attempt to show relief on the map by means of shading.

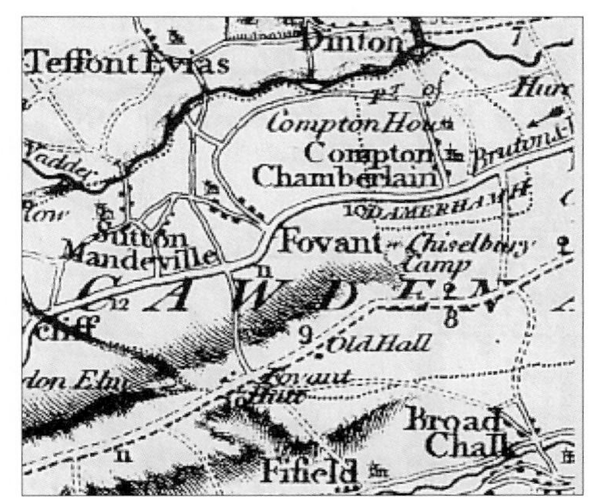

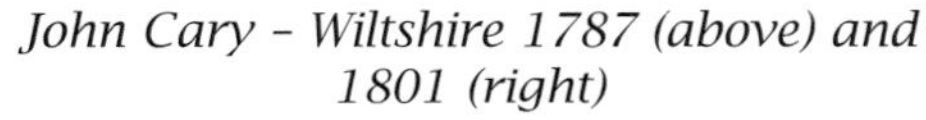
John Cary - Wiltshire 1787 (above) and 1801 (right)

John Cary, who was born near Warminster, left Wiltshire to become an apprentice to a London engraver in 1770. Whilst Fovant is shown as little more than a blob and the village roads are not as detailed as in the Andrews & Dury map, it is clear that the turnpike road passing Chiselbury was considered to be equally as important as the road nearer to the village, which became a turnpike in the same year that the map was produced.

Some 14 years after his earlier work, John Cary produced *Cary's New English Atlas.* Whilst the road pattern of Fovant is now clearer, it is still not as detailed as the Andrews & Dury map of 28 years earlier. The new turnpike is shown as prominently as the old one passing Chiselbury. Between Fovant Hut and Chiselbury is marked Old Hall, of which there is now no trace. This map also shows the physical relief of the landscape, which the intervening maps since Andrews & Dury have not attempted.

Christopher Greenwood was a Yorkshireman who, with partners, published an atlas of most of the English and Welsh counties in 1820. This map shows much more detail than previous maps. There are considerably more houses, the Pembroke Arms inn is shown and the road pattern can easily be traced on a modern map. Shading has again been used to indicate the lie of the land.

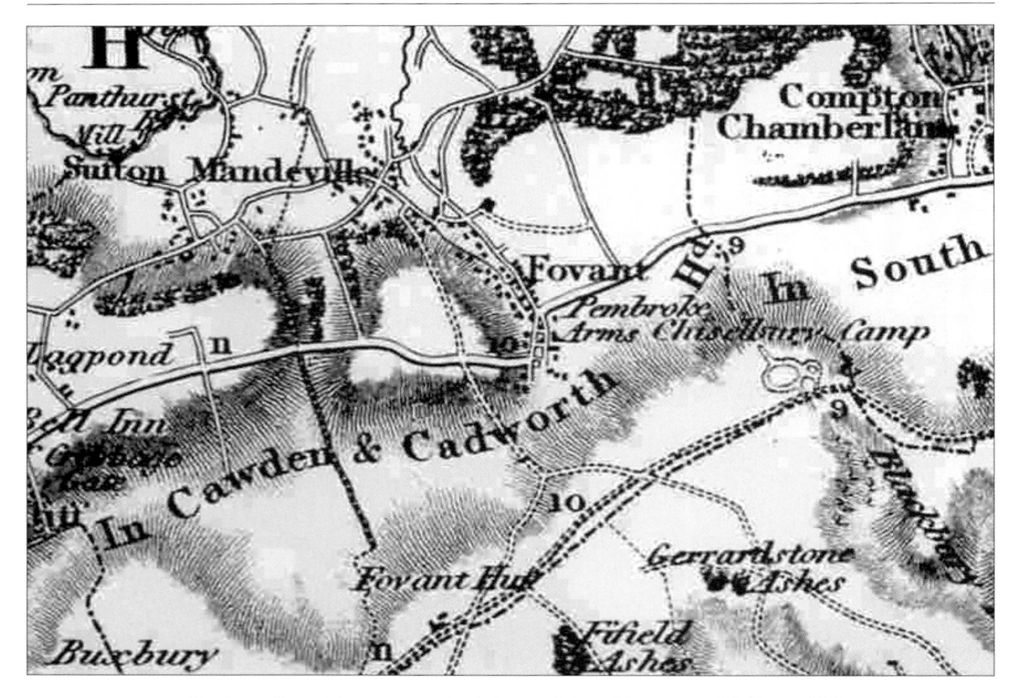

Christopher Greenwood - Map of the County of Wilts 1820

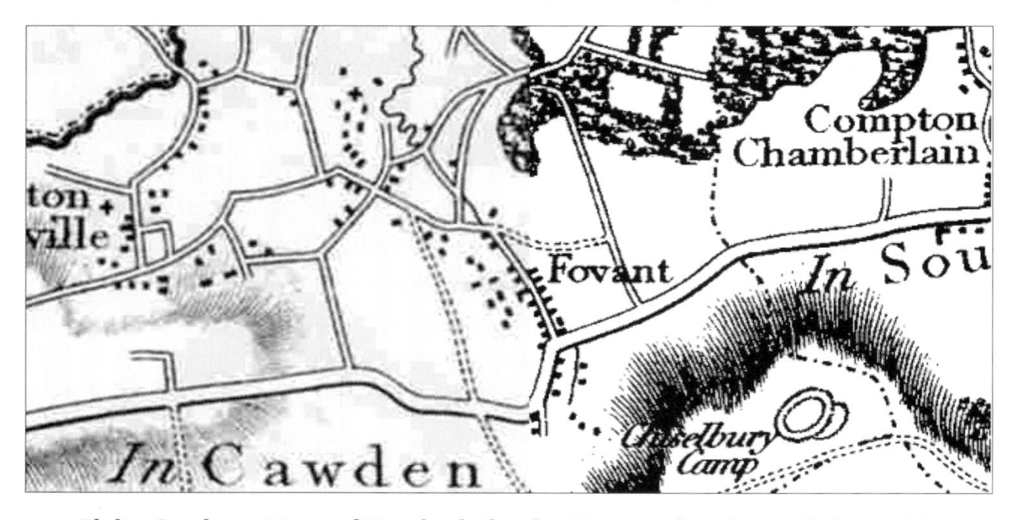

Philip Crocker - Maps of Hundreds for the History of Modern Wiltshire 1829

Philip Crocker, of Frome, followed his father as a land surveyor and from 1805 to 1812 he was one of four civilian surveyors employed by the Ordnance Survey. The maps are of a very high standard. Houses are represented separately, the roads appear to be accurately placed and the form of shading known as hachuring, which gives a clear impression of the physical features, depicts the landscape.

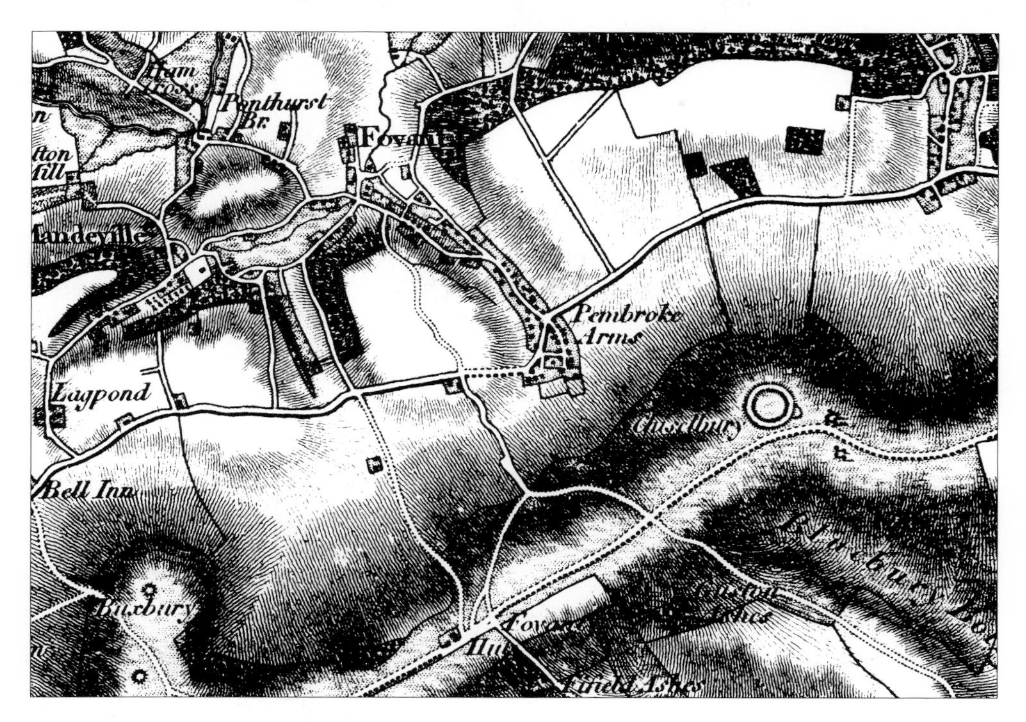

Ordnance Survey – First Edition 1811

The survey into our area started in 1794 and, after the maps were drawn and engraved, Sheet 15, named Salisbury, was first published in 1811. Later editions added more detail, including railways, but the example shown is the map in its earliest state.

Turnpike roads

THE OLD TURNPIKE, which runs along the top of the downs, variously named as The Turnpike on Salisbury Plain, The Ten Mile Course and The Great Western Post Road, is now a byway and has previously been mentioned as The Herepath. How old it is we do not know. It certainly did not exist in 500 BC when the Early Iron Age village at Fifield Ashes was in being, for the lynchets of that period ran right across the crest of the downs. A turnpike gate opposite Chiselbury was shown on Andrew & Dury's map of 1773, and at some date which is not known, the gate was removed to Fovant Hut.

In 1725 the Earl of Pembroke placed numbered milestones along the road and planted a tree by the side of each 'to make them more observable'. Although the milestones have long disappeared, several lime trees at about the right intervals can still be seen, nearer to Wilton. Unfortunately, none has been identified near Fovant.

In February 1768 a petition from 'the gentlemen and inhabitants of the neighbourhood' was sent to Parliament, asking that the use of the old road should be discontinued and that the lower road 'from Barford new bridge through Fovant to White Sheet Hill' should become the official coach road. This road, which had been made in 1702, became The Turnpike under Salisbury Plain in 1787. The Cross Keys inn was the headquarters of The Trustees of the Turnpike, but they soon moved to the Glove Inn at Donhead. The so-called 'Fovant gate', was situated on the Fovant-Compton Chamberlayne boundary, where there was a house which is marked on the Enclosure map. 'Tailor' Foyle was the last gatekeeper. Other gates were at Wilton and at The Glove, Donhead. The charges were 4½d. per carriage and 1½d. for the rider of a horse.

Other roads and paths

MANY OF THE ROADS shown on the map still exist and in 1928 Dr Clay described their history.

He thought that **Green Drove** was probably an extension of the Sigewine's Dyke that we last met in the Anglo-Saxon Charter. Its continuation now becomes Catherine Ford Hill, passing Sandy Hollow, to continue northwards, with Early Iron Age encampments on its flanks.

A bridle way now runs from the Tisbury Road, through Touching Head Copse, southwards to cross the present A30 at Scotland Buildings, then southwards to the foot of the downs. In 1787 the Enclosure Award called this the **Limbway**. From the A30 it becomes a road, sometimes called **The Hollow-way,** which climbs the downs and bears left about 100 yards short of the crest. To the right, a track ran to the turnpike gate at Fovant Hut, then across the Old Turnpike to Ebbesborne Wake. The left fork, now the present road, continues over the crest to Fifield Bavant.

At the foot of the downs there was another branch road, running in a south-easterly direction up the slope, over the crest and down to the village of Broad Chalke. This is now a byway.

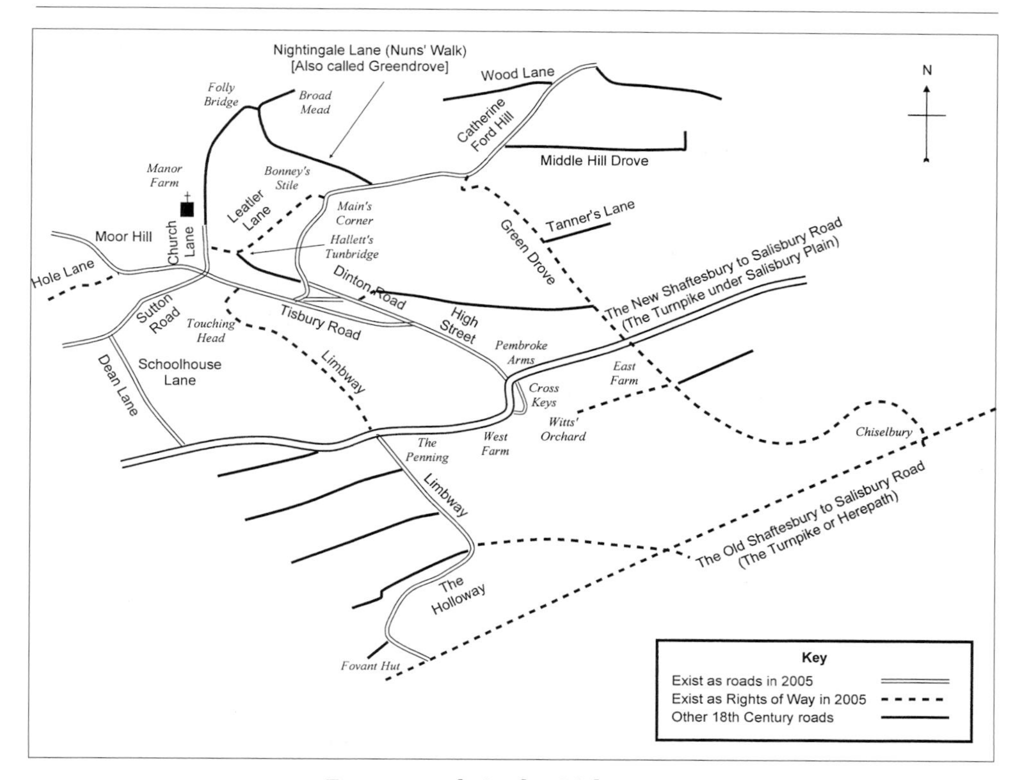

Fovant roads in the 18th century

Formerly, **Dean Lane** continued southwards across the present A30 to the foot of the downs and then up the slope to Fovant Hut. This is now just a footpath. In the other direction it merged into Sutton Road and Church Lane and ended at Manor Farm, just below the church. Nowadays a footpath leaves Church Lane to cross the stream and follow the line of the old bridleway to Teffont Mill.

The names of other roads have been forgotten, but this is how Dr Clay remembered them in 1928. Many of the field names that he mentioned have also been forgotten, but they can be found on the Enclosure Award maps on page 11.

The maps of 1787 and 1811 show a branch road at the bottom of Catherine Ford Hill running due east under Compton Woods to link up with a road called **Horseshoe Lane**. On the opposite side of Catherine Ford Hill, but higher up the slope, another road branched westwards in the direction of Teffont Mill.

The map of 1787 shows a **Mansion Lane** leading from the bridge over the stream in front of the Manor House, made between 1773 and 1787, to meet the present Dinton Road at the top of Mill Lane. Another road, **Leatler Lane**, ran from the bridge to Main's Corner (the sharp corner on the road to Dinton) and on as the present road. In 1811 Mansion Lane was still a highway, but Leatler Lane had become a footpath.

About 150 yards east of Main's Corner, **Nightingale Lane**, (which in 2004 is the road leading down to the sewage treatment plant), was a highway down to Folly Bridge. The same road was sometimes called **Nun's Walk.**

Wood Lane ran due west from the bottom of Catherine's Ford Hill to end in the wood near the field known as Old Russell's and, in the opposite direction, a road ran along the north edge of Fovant Wood to Compton Chamberlayne.

Middle Hill Drove ran from the middle of Catherine Ford Hill due east, along the south edge of Summer Ground and then down the east side of it.

Tanner's Lane was a road running due east from the middle of the Green Drove.

A bridleway was shown as running from Witt's orchard southwards to the foot of the downs, where it turned to the southwest and ascended the slope, to make a junction with the top of the present eastern branch of the end of Limbway. This bridleway is still in existence.

Dr Clay wrote that **Cricketers' (or Crickety) Steps** began at the foot of the downs at the end of that bridleway. He thought that they were cut by Fovant shepherds who had frequently to climb the downs to tend their sheep.

He was also told by a very old man that, according to his grandmother, the women living in the upper part of the village used to go up these steps to reach the patch of land called the Poor Gorse, situated on top of the downs to the west of the eastern arm of Limbway. There they cut faggots of 'Fuzz' or gorse for their bread ovens.

Despite an extensive search, the 'steps' could not be distinguished in 2002.

Waywardens

A 'Statute for the Mending of Highways' in 1555 required each parish to appoint two persons to act as 'Surveyors of Highways' and acceptance of this duty was compulsory. In Fovant these persons were known as Waywardens and the following extracts from their later accounts give some idea of the tasks that they undertook:

Year	Amount	Entry	Comment
1783	£1. 13s. 3½d.	To 2 Way Rates that the Rev Eyre refused to pay	A surprising entry
1789	5 shillings	John Jay's bill for putting up Bright's Bridge	It appears that John Jay's work was not very lasting
	1 shilling	To Mr Goodfellow for mending the bridge	
1803	£3. 16s. 4d.	Turnpike money	The length of the Turnpike road was recorded as 1 mile 5 furlongs 5 chains 2½ yards
1808	£7. 13s. 4d.	Turnpike money	In this year there was an agreement with the commissioners for repairing the turnpike road for 7 years @ £ 10 per mile each year
1817	£19. 15s. 1d.	Recd. of Mr South, The Glove, Donhead, for 1 year's repairing of turnpike	The Glove was the headquarters of the Trustees
		Women @ 6d. per day, Men @ 1s .0d. per day	Clearly both sexes were involved in turnpike maintenance
1817	3s. 6d.	Mr Stevens, for beer 'at the drain near the field'	It was also thirsty work!
1782	1s. 6d.	Mending the wheelbarrow	Inevitably, tools were often replaced
1805	4s 8d.	A spade	
1806	2s. 6d.	A shovel	
1819	£1. 3s. 6d.	2 pickaxes and 3 shovels	
1783	10 shillings	For cleaning the river	The rivers were often mentioned
1795	5d.	Opening the watercourse	
1803	£20	To Mr Barnes for putting up the Catherine Ford bridge	
1818	7 shillings	For cleaning the river below the bridge	

Then and Now

It is possible to compare many of the geographical features that are present now with those that were visible to our predecessors. The landscape is constantly adapted to the needs of employment, building and leisure, but under the surface the rocks remain. Much of the present parish boundary still follows the line established by the Saxons. Field names, or even house names, can relate to the enclosures established in the eighteenth century. Maps now employ satellite and digital technology, but their aims are still those of Andrews, Dury and others of their period. Turnpikes may come back, but meanwhile, by exploring other roads, byways, bridleways and footpaths, we can visualise what travel may have been like and see that surfaces still have to be maintained, rivers cleared and bridges built. Waywardens live on.

M.C.L.H.

3
People

IN A HEAVILY WOODED Nadder Valley, before any established settlements existed, there were many prehistoric visitors to the area we now refer to as Fovant parish. These were hunter-gatherers who followed seasonal but well-trodden paths in pursuit of deer, but also supplemented a varied diet with fish, wild fowl, nuts and berries and even aquatic plants.

Within the current Fovant parish boundary, where Fovant Brook joins the River Nadder, there is an area where family groups from the later Mesolithic period of perhaps 7,500 years ago once returned year upon year. In the knowledge that they could source food here and build shelters from an abundant supply of hazel, they also brought with them the all-important flint that was so vital to sustain life throughout prehistory. Flint provides a means of creating fire and making essential tools such as knives, projectiles, points and scrapers. These early toolmakers would be seated as they carried

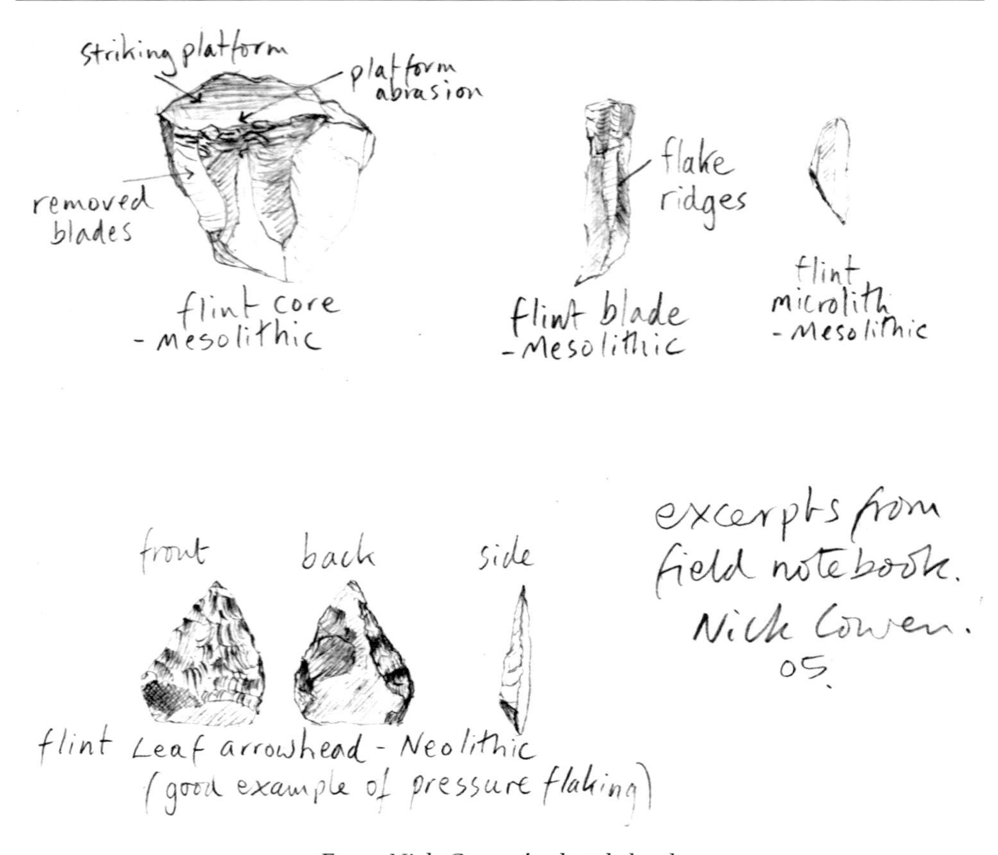

From Nick Cowen's sketch book

out this everyday task, with the flint waste dropping to the floor about their feet. Occasionally the finished tools can be retrieved from the soil at these locations, but more usually it is the knapping waste that provides the evidence of life here all those years ago.

At Fir Hill and, indeed, across the broad belt of Upper Greensand in Fovant and the neighbouring villages, there is a huge amount of this flint-knapping debris and also discarded tools manufactured from imported flint, lying in the soil. Importantly, due to variations in flint-knapping technology, the successive eras of prehistory can be identified with some accuracy. The evidence here reflects a continuity of occupation from the seasonal Mesolithic visitors through to the establishment of early farming and settlement in the Neolithic period. The widespread clearance of trees continued into the Bronze Age as more land was made available for farming. With an abundance of spring water, in combination with the well-drained

Upper Greensand soil, which is ideal for cultivation, and the nearby pastoral chalk downland, there is little wonder that life prospered here.

Inevitably, as the prehistoric population expanded, the pressure on land-use increased. Local strongholds became necessary and in the Early Iron Age small circular defensive structures were built, such as at Chiselbury, which would have offered a retreat in times of unrest. During the unsettled years towards the end of the Iron Age, larger tribal units were formed and smaller hillforts were replaced by vast and heavily-defendable regional hillforts, such as Old Sarum. The nearest large hillfort in our area is that at Castle Ditches near Tisbury, although, at the time of the Roman invasion, the northern tribal boundary of the region was the Grovely ridge.

After the Roman occupation, Old Sarum became a crossing point for two major roads. One route headed north of the river Nadder and thence west towards the Bath area, and the other, after crossing the Ebble to the south, led on to the coastal area of Hamworthy. According to the Ordnance Survey map of Roman Britain, several minor occupation sites existed in the large area sandwiched between these two roads.

Of these sites, one noted as '*possibly of Roman date*' was in the proximity of our future village, so settlement of a kind appears to have been in the Fovant/Sutton Mandeville area at that time.

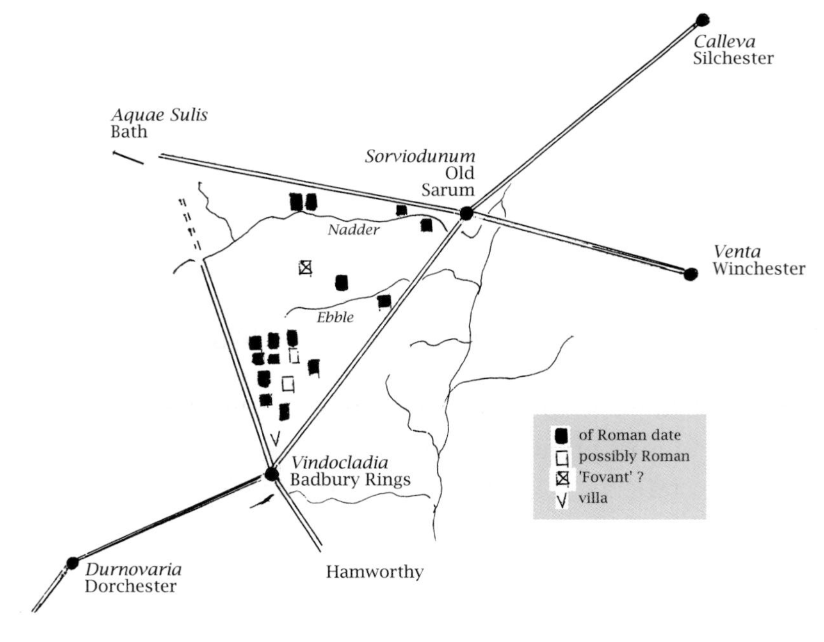

Map of Romano-British settlement in the Fovant area

The discovery in 1967 of a Romano-British bust set into a wall niche in Chapel Cottage, Sutton Row, Sutton Mandeville, suggests a settlement of some social standing. Since the bust, thought to be a portrait, is carved in local stone, it is also reasonable to assume that local craftsmen in considerable numbers were employed.

Romano-British bust from Sutton Mandeville

Some smaller finds were made in the Chiselbury area and there is some suggestion that Romano-British shepherds tended their flocks on our Downs. Additionally, in the course of some construction work along the slope of Fir Hill above Dinton Road, three stone burial cists of the period were unearthed:

> The cists had more or less collapsed over the centuries so the skeletons within were in poor condition. The only relics found were several hobnails commonly used by the Romano-British, and part of a large pot-bellied vessel of hard grey ware. One of the skeletons had a tibia broken in life and healed with a 1½ inch overlap. The one good skull showed evidence of a large hooked nose and 7 remaining teeth (the rest having been lost during her rather long life.) It was determined as being of a woman long past middle age with very worn teeth from eating coarse food, but they had no decay'.
> *(from an article by G.H.Engleheart. Vol.XXXIX. WANH magazine).*

It seems highly likely that these remains are of people who were residents of what would in time become the village of Fovant.

It was not until the early Middle Ages that the village in the valley really came into being. The invading Saxons, after possibly landing at Southampton Water, pushed their way west, establishing settlements in their wake. Fovant is one of the many riverside villages they founded and it is from Fobbefunta, the fountain of/belonging to Fobbe, the Saxon name for the village, that the current name is derived. Was Fobbe then the first named

Fobbe – Saxon chieftain or a water deity

resident of Fovant...or was he/she/it a deity associated with the fountain?

Saxon Land Charter of 901 A.D. concerned the lands of Fovant and Sutton Mandeville, which King Eadward granted to the thegn Wihtbrord. The *Concise Oxford Dictionary* defines 'thegn' as 'one holding land from the king by military service', so Wihtbrord was likely to have been a soldier of some considerable rank. Apart from this second naming of a resident, the charter gave a very clear picture of land boundaries but no further mention was made of the other inhabitants of the village.

In their turn the Normans, after their invasion of 1066, were equally interested in investigating the bounds of their newly-acquired territory. Unlike the Saxons, who only listed land boundaries, the Normans also made an inventory of all the goods and chattels the land contained. Consequently, by 1087 a register listing all this information, known as the Domesday Book, was produced. Fovant has a brief mention in this book, but as far as the population is concerned it is merely noted as having '*seven free men, eight villagers and seven bordars.'*

Ipsa æccla ten FEBEFONTE . T . R . E . geldb p . x . hid . Tra . e vii . car . De hac tra st in dnio . v . hidæ . 7 ibi . ii . car . 7 vii . colibti . Ibi . viii . uilli 7 vii . bord cu . v . car . Ibi . ii . molini redd . xvii . sol . 7 vi . den . 7 viii . ac pti . Pastura . iiii . qz lg . 7 una qz lat . Silua . ii . qz lg . 7 una qz lat . Val . vii . lib 7 x . sol .

"Fovant. Before 1066 it paid tax for 10 hides. (1 hide = 120 acres). Land for 7 ploughs. Of this land 5 hides in lordship; 2 ploughs there; 7 freedmen. 8 villagers and 7 smallholders with 5 ploughs. 2 mills which pay 17s 6d; meadow, 8 acres; pasture 4 furlongs long and 1 furlong wide; woodland 2 furlongs long and 1 furlong wide. Value £7 10s."

Much more useful for our purpose of seeing the residents of Fovant as people rather than statistics, are the records of the successive Earls of Pembroke, whose archives are now kept at the County Record Office in Trowbridge. Wilton House, the seat of the Earl of Pembroke and Montgomery, was built on land given to the Herbert family by Henry VIII after the Dissolution of the Monasteries in the early 16th century. The family also acquired many of the villages of the surrounding area, one of which was Fovant. Manorial surveys followed and it is from these very detailed lists of what property the village contained, who lived where, and how much rent or service each person owed to the Earl, that we get our first knowledge of the people of the village and the sort of life they lived.

Wilton House - seat of the Earls of Pembroke

As can be seen from this small extract from the Manor Court rolls, selected from various entries made between 1742 and 1820, every aspect of the villager's life was prescribed. Attendance at the annual Manor Courts, usually held at the Cross Keys, was mandatory and backsliders in this respect were fined:

All the freeholders, leaseholders and copyholders of this Manor who owe suit and service at the court and have this day made default in not appearing and do amerce (fine) them each as follows, to wit: freeholders 6d., leaseholders 1s.0d., copyholders 2s.6d. each and so assessed.

George Hulott to continue as Hayward for the year ensuing.

A new erected cottage be set up by Robert Day in the Common Ground of the Manor without leave (permission) of the lord of the Manor.

William Goodfellow being dead since the last general court. . . his copyhold to be held by his wife Ann for her widowhood.

William Young (to be presented) for not keeping up and maintaining a gate belonging to Broadmead Common. . . ordered to be repaired within a week under penalty of 10s.0d.

All the villagers were Pembroke tenants, who rented not only their cottages but also, in varying degrees, land of some kind or another. Some tenants were obviously of higher standing than others and as such their holdings were listed in some detail. For instance in the Pembroke Land Survey of 1632:

Robert Feltham holds by indenture...the capital messuage or farm place of Fovant manor for his life; rent £7.13s, 4d, and 6qr, of oats; remainder to John Feltham for life at the same rent. To which a dwelling house of 4 ground rooms lofted over, 2 barns of 12 rooms, 2 stables, an ox house with other necessary house for husbandry, an orchard and a hopyard, meadows called Uckers Mead, Glides Mead and Oddy Mead, closes called Stewards Mead and Home Close, 120 acres of arable called Alldeane, closes of Arable called Broom Close, Timber Hayes, Wood Close, a parcel of arable called Furzy Hill Grove and another called Heathy Down; with common pasture for 16 horses, 33 other beasts and 360 sheep Worth £120.

Robert Feltham was undoubtedly a very wealthy man, as were the thirty-seven other tenants by indenture or copy, whose names and details of their holdings follow those of Robert's. Unlike these more 'landed' tenants, most Fovant villagers rented a small cottage which usually had a large garden in which vegetables would be grown.

Some of the field names can be tied to actual people who feature in some of these records - Goodfellow's Coppice, Hickman's Orchard, Nightingale's Main. Farms were named after their owners - Gerrard's Farm,

Ing's Farm. Small groups of village housing use village surnames in their titles - Jay's Folly, Wyatt's Orchard and Clay's Orchard..

One of our roads, Mary Barter's Lane, is named after a past resident. During the 17th century, there were six ladies of this name and one each in the 18th and 19th centuries respectively. Which of them could the lane have been named for? Those of the 17th century are unlikely candidates. She of the 18th century is a possibility, for she was the daughter of the miller, and the mill was situated at the bottom of the lane. Alternatively, it could have been the Mary born in 1820, who, according to Doctor Clay, lived in a cottage at the junction of Mill Lane with Mansion Lane. For the first time we have a wealth of names, some of which, Martyn, Jay, Nightingale, Jarvis, Strong, Goodfellow, Barter and indeed Feltham, will keep cropping up.

Parish registers of births, marriages and deaths only became a legal requirement in 1837, but Bishop's Registers which listed baptisms and burials, started in 1209. Similarly, many parishes kept marriage registers well before the legal requirement to do so. The Wiltshire Family History Society, which publishes extracts from the Bishop's Transcripts and Parish Registers, has covered Fovant baptisms and burials from 1541-1837.

In the decade 1540-50 alone, several baptisms are noted for children of the Barter, Feltham, Nightingale and Martyn families, and burials for the same period reflect the same family names. Our earliest recorded headstone is for Grace Jay, wife of Thomas, born 1688, died 1770. The inscriptions on many of these early headstones are indecipherable, but some can be discerned by use of a brass-rubbing technique.

Fovant marriage registers also date from 1541. During this very early period, familiar surnames such as Barter, Strong, Feltham, Hayward, Nightingale and Martyn often feature. By the 19th century, however, many of these names have disappeared, to be replaced by more currently familiar surnames like Wyatt, Goodfellow, Hardiman, Lever, Jarvis, Simper, Coombs or Jay.

Fovant Church Memorials, a book produced in the village in 1997, not only identifies gravestone positions, but also notes all burials from 1942 when the current register was started. It also includes details of the wall-mounted memorial plaque inside the church, which contains not only the names of village men who fell during WWI, but also those who returned safely. Additionally, the names of casualties from both WWI and WWII are engraved on our War Memorial outside the Village Hall. Twenty-two of our

Village Hall War Memorial reminds us of the cost of war

men are remembered on this memorial, many of whose surnames are still familiar in the village today.

Memorial seats have also proved popular. Scattered throughout the village, they largely commemorate people who are buried in our churchyard. Occasionally, however, a seat is dedicated to a past resident who, although their last resting place lies elsewhere, has had some long lasting affection for Fovant. It is as though they had come home.

Memorial plaque for a past resident

The need for a new Visitors' Book in the church has, by giving us the chance to study the old book, made available a previously unsuspected historical reference source. Covering the period from the 14th March 1978 to the 14th July 2003, the entries provide us with a quarter of a century of details of people who have visited our church. Many of these people have made several visits. Their ages cover a wide range and they come from near and far - local, national and international. Their reasons for coming are manifold, varying from grieving relatives, those tracing ancestors, former residents, children evacuated to Fovant during World War II, to those who were born, christened, confirmed, or married here.

Many visitors have commented on the beauty of the church's setting and the feeling of tranquillity that prevails, while others have noted the reason for their visit. Although we are appreciative of the complimentary remarks about our church and its venue, it is the reasons for the visits which are of major interest to us. The selection from the remarks made in the 'comment' column of the recently-completed Church Visitors Book noted below, illustrates clearly the yearning to return felt by many of our Fovant 'exiles':

> *'Rest peacefully now you are home in Fovant'* - three daughters remember their mother, who, having died elsewhere, was buried in her 'own' churchyard.
>
> *'I was a child here and love to come back'* - now living in America.
>
> *'I miss it'* - child whose parents moved away.
>
> *'Memories of our wedding day in 1944'* - now living in America, a local girl who married an American serviceman?
>
> *'Evacuated here during the war'* - three ladies from London.
>
> *'My great, great, great grandfather was married in this church'* - visitor from Australia.

Several local children, perhaps at a loose end during the school holidays, have visited more than once. Innocently earnest as small children, in impeccably neat, childish writing, we get such remarks as '*I prayed for my sister*' or '*a very nice place*'. A few years later the writing has gone haywire, naughtiness has set in and, having entered their own name in the right place, they sign silly names in the comment column. Later still come the anguished adolescents with '*please make it come right God*' and '*I won't come to church*

WWII identity card, which had to be carried at all times

again'. Finally, they come as adults, with their own children.

Perhaps the most useful source for the identification of the individuals who have made up Fovant's 19th century population are the Census schedules. The national census of England and Wales was first taken in 1801 and, with the exception of 1941, when the wartime issuing of National Registration Identity Cards in effect constituted a census, has been taken every ten years since.

At the time of the first census in 1801, Fovant's population numbered 514. In 1991 the figure stood at 641. Although the figure for Fovant's population evened out over this period, the accompanying table and graph show two instances when the figures involved showed a large change in the statistics.

Firstly, from 1851 to 1901, there was a general decline in the population, which is probably associated with the opening of the Salisbury and Yeovil

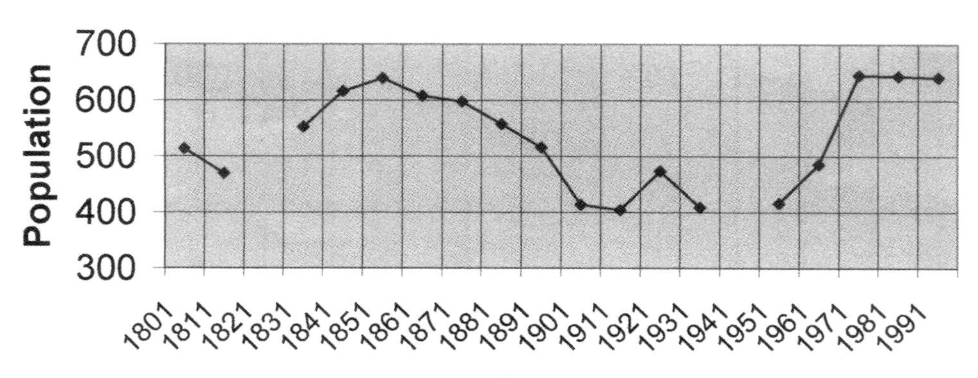

Railway Company, which had a station at Dinton. Undoubtedly, better, cheaper public transport encouraged the young to explore further afield. Secondly, that the reverse situation could also have applied is indicated by the temporary 'blip' between 1961 and 1981, when the population increased by approximately 150. This was almost certainly due to the 'infilling' house building that occurred during this period.

Minimal social information was contained in the earlier Census schedules, but the questionnaire was gradually broadened, so that by 1851 the returns had to include address, Christian and surname, indication of head of household, marital state, relationship to head, gender, age, occupation and place of birth. Goodfellow, Read, Jay, Coombes, Wyatt, Foyle and Simper, all surnames which feature in the early Census returns, are still represented in the village today.

A direct relationship cannot always be traced between people with the same surname, but family bibles and papers have proved invaluable when trying to do so. Amongst such documents have been:

Bessie Louise Young (b.1875) - future wife of George Lever

The 19th century quit rent account for Fovant Wood, made out to Henry Simper, from the Earl of Pembroke's estate office.

A copy of the diary of William Simper, who, between 3rd August 1870 and 23rd February 1872, worked on the building of the Canadian Pacific Railway.

Extracts from the daily working diary of Charles Turner, for 1899-1900.

Photographs of ancestors, with names and dates on the reverse.

That some of the families from the earliest records - Feltham, Barter, Nightingale, Martyn - have moved elsewhere is not unusual, for even within an apparently enclosed rural economy there has always been quite a lot of movement. One has only to look at the birth places noted on the

George Lever (1875-1916), lost at sea during the Battle of Jutland. Buried in Norway.

census returns to realise, not only how often people changed their place of employment, but also how far many of them travelled from their birth area. In some cases families can be followed throughout the Census schedules, from the earliest up to 1901.Thereafter, because of the 100-year privacy restriction, we must wait for each following decade before successive 20th century social details are released.

However, much can be gleaned from listening to the childhood memories of our older villagers. The children of the 1901 census, parents and grandparents in their turn, have responded willingly to the question 'what was it like when you were young?' Recorded interviews with

Wedding of Alfred Raymond to Bessie ? in the early 1930s

Alice Maud Turner with some of her children, Charles, Phyllis, Ethel, Doris, Frank and Gwen, in the garden of their house, Sunnyside, in Back Street. Early 1920s.

representatives of the Turner, Wyatt, Green, Foyle, Burton, Lee, Simper, Hardiman and Coombs families, telling of their lives in early 20th century Fovant, have the added bonus of the authentic Wiltshire accent. The importance of such oral evidence cannot be overstated - there is nothing to equal the account of someone who was there, given in the words of an eyewitness. Each little piece of information gives us an insight into the Fovant of the past, helping to bridge the gap between ancestors and descendants.

Now in 2005, the population is obviously considerably larger than it was when the village in the valley was first settled. In the years between then and now, some people have moved into the area, others have moved out and many have stayed put. It is of no consequence which of these categories our residents through the ages fall within; all, from the prehistoric people making the flint implements found on Fir Hill, to the newest-come babe amongst us, are villagers, the people of Fovant.

J.O.H.

4
Buildings

Introduction

ALTHOUGH OUR VILLAGE was first settled in Saxon times, it was not until the early 17th century, when the earliest stone cottages were built, that the Fovant seen today began to take shape. Most of the houses are situated along the High Street, Tisbury Road and Dinton Road. There are some small terraces, but most of the houses are detached. Many houses are built end-on to the road, making the most of the space in the narrow valley. Fovant has some listed buildings, including Fovant House and Fovant Elm on Church Lane, Oakhanger Barn on the High Street and the Pembroke Arms on the A30.

Much of the parish belonged to successive Earls of Pembroke and Montgomery from the Wilton Estate. However, following the death of the

14th Earl (Sidney Herbert), the Estate was severely hit by death duties and was forced to sell property in several outlying villages, including Fovant, Broadchalke and Wishford. A public auction was held on 27 August 1919 and the Fovant sale consisted of 89 lots (approximately 2,067 acres). The sale particulars show that the Fovant estate included dairy farms, smallholdings, cottages, allotments and several potential building sites.

The sale particulars provide valuable information about many of the houses we can see in the village today. For example, West Farm was described as a dairy and sheep farm of approximately 584 acres. The sale included withy beds, West Farm House with seven bedrooms, a pair of cottages, Scotland Buildings and Fovant Hut. At the time of the sale, the farm was let to Mr H Hitchings. Buildings half way up Green Drove, part of East Farm, were described as, '*a modern homestead*' comprising: north range, with root house, cooling house, wagon lodge, double cow house to tie twelve cows; east range, comprising of a cow house to tie fourteen cows; and west range, with space for seventeen cows. East Farm was sold with part of Fovant Down and Chiselbury Camp. The farmhouse was described as a '*well built stone and tiled residence standing in a good position having a south and west aspect overlooking the village and Fovant Downs.*' The house was made up of five bedrooms with six attic bedrooms.

Other sale particulars are available to view at the Wiltshire & Swindon Record Office. In 1910, the lease on Fishponds (now The Rectory) was sold on behalf of James Futcher. The house was described as a '*newly erected detached residence with garden and tennis court.*' The old Rectory, Church Lane, which was renamed 'Fovant House' after being sold in 1949 with fifteen acres, was described as of stone construction with a tiled roof. The front elevation is late 17th or early 18th century and the rear portion dates to Tudor times. After another recent name

Fishponds, our current Rectory

The Old Rectory

change the house is now called 'The Old Rectory'. The Manor House, also on Church Lane, was sold in 1972 by the widow of Dr R.C.C. Clay. The front of the house is described as mid-16th century and the rear as 18th century. It was used as a doctor's surgery from around 1850.

A walk around the village today reveals extensive use of stone as a building material. This greensand is probably from a local quarry, maybe even Fovant's own quarry that was situated in a field north of the Pembroke Arms.

The stone cottages of the village vary widely in size, design and date and architecturally fall into the category known as vernacular. As architects were rarely, if ever, employed in vernacular building, the likelihood of the existence of dated individual plans or records is minimal. Almost certainly the building of the cottages in Fovant was the work of local craftsmen, as many masons and carpenters are to be found in the census returns.

Dating these stone buildings, though problematical, is not impossible. Until roughly the middle of the 17th century, most rural cottages tended to be flimsily constructed, one-room hovels that fell into disrepair within a generation or two. It seems unlikely, therefore, that many of our cottages predate that period. Since virtually all of Fovant's inhabitants were Pembroke tenants, records exist of some of the buildings in the village. In the Pembroke Survey for 1631-32 for instance, the farmhouse of Edward

Barter is described as '*a dwelling house of four ground rooms, two of them lofted over*'. There was also '*a barn of three rooms*'. This could well have been the house at the top of Mary Barter Lane that was still in existence in the early 20th century. Also in Fovant, John Hannam held '*a cottage newly erected of two rooms and a little garden and orchard adjoining*' for an annual rent of sixpence.

Building Reports

FOLLOWING FIELD DAYS held by the Wiltshire Buildings Record (Trowbridge), more has been learnt about the structure and approximate dates of certain buildings in the village.

Baker's Cottage

One of the end-on cottages in the High Street, Baker's Cottage was the subject of an investigation in June 2001. The report states:

> This stone cottage probably dates from about 1600 and is a very good example of a 2-room end stack plan. It was originally 1½ storeys high with a single light window in the stack wall at the top of the stair to light the loft area. It was probably thatched. The original stonework is almost in chequers with, in places, a square of small rubble stones between larger stones. The house was raised to a full 2 storeys in height in the early 19th century.

Springfield

Also in June 2001, members of the Wiltshire Buildings Record looked at Springfield, situated in Mill Lane. They concluded that '*the development of the house is difficult to interpret because of later alterations*'. The original building was probably late 17th century, suggested by the main stack and the crossbeam in the main room. '*The house was probably 1½-storeys high at this date.*' During the 18th century the roof was raised and the house extended to the west to form a sizeable two-storey farmhouse with a parlour. New windows and roof were fitted in the 19th century. More recently a large extension to the south-east has been added, virtually doubling the size of the property.

The 1840 Tithe Map shows a continuous range of agricultural outbuildings extending along the edge of the property to the east. The 1923

Ordnance Survey map shows that these buildings had been removed by this time.

Cross Keys House, once part of the Hotel, now a private residence

Cross Keys House

Although Cross Keys House is now a private residence, it was previously part of the Cross Keys inn. The ground floor wall thickness, of at least 24 ins, suggests a probable early 17th century origin.

> The chamfered mullions of the ground floor differ from the ovolo-moulded mullions of the first floor suggesting the house may have been raised in height in the late 17th century. . . A small stone extension behind the house may have originated as a stair turret when the house was 1½ rather than 2 storeys high.

In the past, there were three main rooms on the ground floor. The room to the north was the kitchen, with a large fireplace and bread oven. The central room would have been unheated and may have included a buttery or dairy.

The current entrance is through a 19th century polygonal bay lobby, but originally the house had a baffle entry. This means that on entering the house, one had to turn either right or left through the lobby to enter the rooms. This would have kept the heat in the main rooms.

The Wiltshire Buildings Record concludes by saying:

> The house is well-built and a substantial size. It is likely to have been a farmhouse in the 17th century whether or not it was an inn or alehouse as well at that time.

The Church of St. George

It is thought that the Saxons built a church on or near the site of the present church, but if this is so, no trace of its existence remains. The current church was built in the 15th century, when the Perpendicular style of architecture prevailed. The framework of the priests' door, leading into the chantry chapel, is a relic of the original Norman church. It was found in fragments in the south wall when the fabric was restored in the 1860s. T.H.Wyatt, the architect, reconstructed it and placed it where it now stands, close to the piscina.

The interior consists of a nave and two side-aisles, with a chantry chapel south of the chancel. The north aisle is separated from the nave by four pointed arches, springing from round columns. The south aisle

St. George's Church

presents only three arches, springing from octangular columns without capitals.

Some of the stonework at the top of the tower was replaced during 1988 by The Cathedral Works Department, Salisbury.

Repairs to the church tower parapet, 1988

Fovant Chapel

The Chapel was officially opened in November 1820 by the Rev. Wm. Jay of Bath, having been founded in 1815 by a group of local people known as 'Dissenters', who began meeting for prayer and worship in a house on the opposite side of the High Street to the present building.

The Chapel

Construction is of local stone with a roof of Welsh slate. Originally the floor area was of bricks laid directly on to Greensand. Downstairs seated about 60 people, with a balcony on the rear and side walls seating another 50. During the 1870s the side balconies were removed and a new wooden floor placed over the original bricks.

In more recent years a small kitchen and toilet have been provided and the original pews have been replaced by a mixture of pews and chairs.

The Inns of Fovant

Fovant Hut

Fovant Hut has also been known as the White Hart Inn or the Hut on Salisbury Plain. It was one of a series of posting houses along the turnpike road, which ran along the ridge of the downs above the village. Although we do not know when the inn was established, the Salisbury and Winchester Journal referred to it as 'new built' in 1757. William Kennell, the first landlord, advertised that he had:

> a stock of neat Wines, rich Cordials, and all sorts of Spirituous Liquors to be sold Wholesale and Retail.

The inn did a thriving trade until 1787 when the Lower Road (now the A30) was turnpiked. It is not known when the inn ceased to trade, but it has long since been a private house.

The Cross Keys

The earliest part of the Cross Keys, situated on the A30, is said to have been built in the late 15th century. Manor Courts were held here between 1724

Cross Keys Hotel, no longer open for business

and 1820, probably in the large room upstairs, which was originally accessed by external stone stairs.

According to the late Olive Mullins, whose grandparents and parents ran the Cross Keys from 1917 to 1942, the stone stairs were removed some time after 1942, possibly because they were an obstruction to traffic on the A30.

The Fovant Club, a sick benefit club mainly for agricultural workers, which was founded in the mid-1700s and ran until 1911, held its meetings in the upstairs room. Meat and vegetables for the Pig Club Suppers were cooked in large coppers situated in the back kitchen. Water had to be fetched from a pump near the Pound, the stone lock-up for stray animals, which used to be near the Brook Street end of the inn.

The Cross Keys closed as an inn on 30 March 2003.

The Pembroke Arms

The Pembroke Arms, opposite the Cross Keys, has been referred to as the Lord's Inn, the Cart Wheel or the Catherine Wheel. The inn was built in the early 1790s, possibly on the site of a previous hostelry. It is of brick and tile construction. The inn was part of lot 81 of the 1919 Pembroke sale and its outbuildings were described as stabling, coach house, cow house and

Pembroke Arms, which houses the museum of WWI memorabilia

piggery. At that time, the inn had a detached garden on the opposite side of the High Street. The stables were demolished after the Second World War, clearing a space for the current car park.

James Millard, the first landlord, informed the public through the local press that he:

> has laid in an assortment of good Old wines and other liquors. Good beds. Well aired . . . neat Post-Chaise with able Horses and careful Drivers.

The beginning of the end for the Poplar Inn

The Poplar Inn

There is some suggestion that the Poplar Inn was at one time called 'The Drum and Monkey', but in 1962 the then owners, Eldridge Pope and Co. disclaimed all knowledge of this name. The date of the building is uncertain, but likely to be between 1789 and 1811. There is no doubt that it was built on an area of ground willed by a Quaker lady to be used as a burial ground for the Brethren, but no documentary or archaeological evidence has proved that it was ever used as such. The Poplar Inn closed in 1998 and the site, in Sutton Road, was used for housing. The area is now known as Home Close.

Doomsday Cottage in the High Street, now demolished

A Village Evolving

THE VILLAGE is constantly changing as houses are demolished, built or extended. Buildings that have been demolished include the Poor House, Hillside, Doomsday Cottages in the High Street (demolished c.1936), Sundial Cottages, also known as the Barracks or Button Factory, near the Village Hall (demolished c.1958), Waterfall Cottages on the Shaftesbury Road (demolished c.1965) and, more recently, The Poplar Inn.

Many dwellings were built in the 1920s and 30s following the Pembroke sale, which made available plots of land, and the closure of Fovant Camp. Building materials from the Camp were advertised in the *Salisbury Journal.* For example:

> '. . . a sale of dismantled hut timber, corrugated iron, and a selected assortment of floorboards, doors, windows, and various timbers. . .'

In 1923, Frank Read, a local builder, built for himself the first bungalow in Fovant, The Croft in Tisbury Road. The following year he built Spring Gardens for Miss Pratt, the school headmistress, and Southlands for

Waterfall Cottage on the Shaftesbury Road, now demolished

his elder brother, both also in Tisbury Road. In 1930 he built Ty Cariad, Forresters and Westdene (now Wesdene) in Dinton Road.

Five bungalows were built along Shaftesbury Road, at the end of Green Drove, by Tom Bracher using materials from the camp. They were built on behalf of John Combes to house his farm workers. One bungalow later fell into disrepair and was replaced in the 1980s.

Old Army huts and corrugated iron roofs were, and in a few cases continue to be, seen within the village. One of these huts was put to very good use by becoming the British Legion Hut. It was placed close to the road in front of what is now Nutwood in Tisbury Road. The hut was officially opened on 16 December 1922. Following frequent use by many groups and individuals, including the Scouts, the Youth Club and people going to dances and whist drives, the hut was sold to a local farmer when the site was developed for housing in 1964.

Another well-used building is the Village Hall which is situated at the junction of Tisbury Road and Dinton Road. The original Church Hall, built on this site in 1885, was destroyed by fire in 1909. It had been built at the instigation of the Rector, the Reverend A. Earle, on land granted to the village by the then Earl of Pembroke. The next church incumbent, the Reverend

M.A.Shorland, organised the building of the current structure in replacement. This current Hall was purchased and renamed by the Parish Council in the 1970s.

Installation of mains water in 1950 and public sewerage in 1962 led to rapid expansion of the village. Weeping Ash in about 1935, The Elms and The Poplars estates in 1952, were built by the Salisbury and Wilton Rural District

The British Legion Hut, removed in 1964 for property development

The Village Hall, venue for many village activities

Clay's Orchard in Sutton Road, providing protected accommodation for the elderly

Council. R.A.F homes were built at Leatler Close in the late 1950s, as married quarters. Clays Orchard (named for Dr R.C.C. Clay) was built in 1969, at the end of Sutton Road, to provide homes for 18 elderly people.

According to the 'Fovant Village Plan', published by the Parish Council in the late 1970s, 43 new dwellings were built between 1968 and 1978. These were mainly placed between existing houses.

In 1989, a village survey was undertaken to ascertain if there was sufficient need in the parish for low-cost housing for Fovant people. The survey showed that there were nearly 300 dwellings at that time. Most respondents indicated a need for new housing, particularly for young people, but it was noted that the amenities, employment opportunities and public transport services available might not be sufficient to attract young people back into the village or to encourage them to stay. The scheme was blighted by the lack of suitable building plots and the problem of affordability, a situation which remains.

Many of the stone cottages have been extended over the years. In some cases extensions have incorporated what were previously outbuildings and barns, as can be seen at Deerhurst, in Brook Street. Agricultural buildings have become dwellings, following changes in farming practice. Examples include Grey Mews at the far end of Church Lane and the buildings in Green Drove, which formerly belonged to East Farm. Although we think of barn conversions as being a modern phenomenon, Greystones, in Green Drove, was converted in the late 1950s.

Some buildings have been altered by sub-division, conversion or extension. Several of what are now semi-detached buildings were previously three dwellings, such as Dene Cottage and Glenlyn on the High Street and Queen's Cottage and Meadow Cottage on Tisbury Road. These show how our ideas of a reasonably-sized house have changed over the years, fuelled by the country's increasing prosperity.

Although most of the buildings consist of private dwellings nowadays, this wasn't always the case. During World War I, a downstairs room of Fovant Elm was used as a small shop and tea room and over the years Fovant has seen many trades and businesses operated from houses or wooden huts in their grounds. Some of these trades live on in the names of current houses, for example The Forge, Fovant Mill, Cobblers, Baker's Cottage and The Malthouse. House names change over the years as owners or circumstances change. We no longer have the names Toads Pond Cottages, Nadder Villa, Fern Cottage or Harts House. Ivy Cottage ceased to be a suitable name once the extensive ivy was removed from what is now October Cottage. Some buildings have changed their function and therefore their names. One example is Fovant House which was previously The Rectory or Parsonage. The change may have been due to decreasing family sizes.

Some house names are indicative of the house's position in the village. For example, Crossing Gate is situated where the railway line used to cross Dinton Road. The ford near Ford Cottage in Brook Street has gone, but the name remains.

Several homes are named after the brook running through the village, for example Brookside Cottage and Brook Cottage. Gunvilles and Home Close recall some of the old field names, while housing developments, such as Sling Orchard or Wyatt's Orchard, might indicate how important cider was to the agricultural worker. The Steps, a bungalow at the lower end of Green Drove, is reached by steps which previously led to the wartime Garrison Cinema.

Conclusion

NOTWITHSTANDING the increased house building that has taken place during modern times, the overall shape and size of the village have changed little over the centuries. Confined not only by its topography, but also by a housing policy which does not permit building beyond its boundaries, the village has expanded by houses being fitted in between existing dwellings. Considerable care has been taken to harmonise the building materials of the new with the old, resulting in an interesting mix of the ancient and modern.

Although Fovant has altered considerably since it was first settled, despite the changes, the shape of the original Saxon street village can still be seen.

S.M.

5
Religion

THERE IS SOME slight evidence of Paganism in the area, connected with an early Bronze Age burial, discovered SW of Chiselbury during an excavation of 1927. Accompanying the remains of a human skeleton, within a wooden coffin, were two red deer antlers. The existence of such grave goods suggests the performance of some form of pagan rites.

During the construction, in 1915, of the light railway serving the Fovant Camps, three stone cists containing skeletons were discovered in an area above the village hall. No relics accompanied these remains, but some large, conical-headed hobnails, identified as Romano-British, were found by the feet of one of the skeletons. Additionally, a large pot, almost certainly Romano-British, stood outside one of the cists. Christianity did arrive in Britain towards the end of the Roman occupation of Britain, but any religious aspect of these burials would almost certainly still have been pagan.

In 1267, the first mention of a church building in Fovant is contained in the will of Robert de Careville, treasurer of Sarum, which says *'...to supplying a deficit in the church at Fofunt, 20 solidos - to the poor of the same parish, 20 solidos'.* A list of Fovant incumbents from 1305, starting with the Norman-sounding name Rob. de Hulcott, indicates that a Christian church existed in the village at this time.

Local historian, Dr Clay, records that the original building was Norman and that the framework of the priest's door, leading into the chantry chapel, is a relic of the original church. He also states that the church was rebuilt in the 15th century in the Perpendicular style. The building of the tower during the incumbency of George Rede (1473 - 1495) is commemorated in a small brass on the chancel wall.

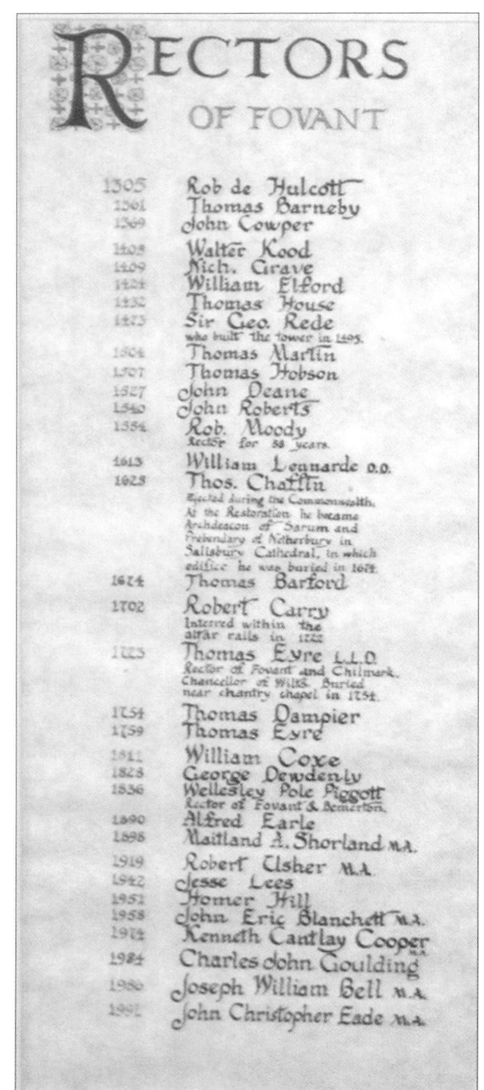

RECTORS OF FOVANT

1305 Rob de Hulcott
1361 Thomas Barneby
1369 John Cowper
1408 Walter Kood
1409 Nich. Grave
1424 William Elford
1432 Thomas House
1473 Sir Geo. Rede
who built the tower in 1495.
1504 Thomas Martin
1507 Thomas Hobson
1527 John Deane
1540 John Roberts
1554 Rob. Moody
Rector for 58 years.
1613 William Leonarde D.D.
1625 Thos. Chaffin
Ejected during the Commonwealth. At the Restoration he became Archdeacon of Sarum and Prebendary of Netherbury in Salisbury Cathedral, in which edifice he was buried in 1678.
1674 Thomas Barford
1702 Robert Carry
Interred within the altar rails in 1722
1725 Thomas Eyre L.L.D.
Rector of Fovant and Chilmark. Chancellor of Wilts. Buried near chantry chapel in 1754.
1754 Thomas Dampier
1759 Thomas Eyre
1811 William Coxe
1823 George Dewdenly
1836 Wellesley Pole Piggott
Rector of Fovant & Bemerton.
1890 Alfred Earle
1898 Maitland A. Shorland M.A.
1919 Robert Usher M.A.
1942 Jesse Lees
1951 Homer Hill
1958 John Eric Blanchett M.A.
1974 Kenneth Cantlay Cooper M.A.
1984 Charles John Goulding
1986 Joseph William Bell M.A.
1991 John Christopher Eade M.A.

Fovant incumbents

The George Rede Brass

When Henry VIII, after an open rift with the Pope, declared himself the Supreme Head of the English Church, the whole country was caught up in the ensuing religious ferment, known as the Reformation.

We must assume that the church in Fovant followed the same path as the rest of the country at this time, albeit more slowly, as befits a rural area where the arrival of news might be delayed. There was a gradual change to the 'Church of England' and the introduction of English instead of Latin for the services, enabling the congregation to understand what was being said, though many of the acts of worship retain their Latin titles to this day, e.g. Nunc Dimittis.

The village of Fovant belonged to Wilton Abbey, one of the wealthiest nunneries in England. In 1539, it became a victim of the King's 'Dissolution of the Monasteries'. The Abbess at the time, Dame Cecily Bodenham, was suspiciously compliant to the king's wishes in this matter, for one of the nuns recorded in her diary:

> Methinks the Abbess hath a faint heart and doth yield up our possessions to the spoiler with a not unwilling haste . . . Master Richard Nevile, the Sub Seneschal, informeth me that His Majesty's Commissioners do purpose to reward her with a fair house at Foffount and a goodly stipend withal.

She was rewarded by the king's commissioners with a stipend of £100 per annum and a house in Fovant. With her to this house, known as the Manor Farm House, came twelve of the nuns from Wilton Abbey. While in Fovant Cicely Bodenham paid for the building of the south aisle of St George's Church, where her coat of arms was still to be seen when John Aubrey visited in the 1670s. Apart from the house, they were given an orchard, gardens and three acres of meadow and one load of wood each year from Fovant woods. The secluded private road from Dinton Road leading towards Church Lane is still called Nun's Walk.

It is said that the area around Wardour contained the largest number of Catholics in the South of England outside London. However, for 200 years following the Reformation it is not clear where Mass was said in the area – probably in private houses or even farm buildings.

The persecution of Catholics, who continued to practise their faith and refused to attend the new church services, occurred in Fovant as it did elsewhere in the country. They were known as Recusants. David Feltham, John Grindle and Amos Barter's widow, who *'secretly kept her beads under her apron',* were among the inhabitants of Fovant who were arrested as suspected Recusants in the middle of the 17th century. At the quarter sessions in Salisbury in January 1643 Edward Lucas, John Lucas, John

St George's Church, showing the South Aisle

Trime and their wives, 'all of Fovant, were presented for being Popish Recusants'.

Additionally J.A.Williams, in his book *Catholic Recusancy in Wiltshire* gives the following list of Fovant Recusants resident during the latter part of the 17th century:

Abbott, James, Quaker, Thatcher.
Abbott, Joan, his wife.
Biddlecombe, Mary, widow, Papist.
Biddlecombe, Ursula, widow, Papist.
Boulde, Elizabeth, widow, Quaker, daughter of Elizabeth Day.
Chappell, George, 'absent from church'
Day, Elizabeth, Quaker.
Day, Margaret, wife of Andrew Day, mercer, daughter of Frances Lucas, Papist.
Dudds, James, 'absent from Church'
Farley, Thomas, described as 'sectary' and absent from Church, 1662-1671, yeoman.

Feltham, Robert, weaver, Dissenter 1662-1678.

Hansom, Henry.

Hansom, John.

Loop, widow.

Lucas, Edward, son of Frances, Papist.

Lucas, Frances, widow, papist.

Lucas, Joan, wife of Edward, daughter of Mary Biddlecome.

Merryweather, Andrew, Quaker.

Merryweather, John, glover, Quaker.

Strong, Elflett, spinster, Papist.

Some of these names are new to us, others have cropped us previously, or will be referred to later. J.A.Williams notes further that

> Martin Biddlecome, alias Edward Coffin, was a secular priest and Vicar-General of the south west of England, from Cornwall to Hampshire. His wife, daughter and daughter-in-law were amongst the most constant 'offenders'.

The list of Fovant incumbents, mentioned earlier, also gives the patrons of the church, which changed from Wilton Abbey in 1554 to Richard Hungerford and then to William Earl of Pembroke in 1613. William had been given the land and the buildings of Wilton Abbey by the King. In 1646 'Parliament' is listed as the patron.

During Cromwell's rule there was a sudden growth in the number of religious sects. Many of them quickly faded from view, but the Quakers survived and, as the Society of Friends, are still with us.

There was an active group of Quakers, or members of the Society of Friends in Truth, in Fovant from the latter half of the 17th to the mid 18th century. They met to worship God on Sundays in each other's homes. Their beliefs in equality, simplicity, honesty, non-violence and silent worship with no priest, meant that they refused to go to church or to pay tithes. For this, fines, seizures of property, floggings or imprisonment were common punishments. Quakers were also refused burial in the churchyard and two were interred in the Pound.

According to the records, in 1661 John Merryweather and his sons, Andrew and John, of Fovant, were apprehended in their house, arrested and taken to Fisherton Gaol in Salisbury together with several other men. Determination to hold to their beliefs eventually paid off for, according to the record of the Quarter Sessions held at Devizes on 14th April 1702,

> The several dwelling houses of Osmond Day and Elizabeth Dunne and James Abbott all of Fovant in the county of Wilts, are set apart and intended to be made use of for the exercise of religious worship by Protestant dissenters called Quakers.

Elizabeth Dunn, in her will dated 1705, left land in Fovant to be used as 'a burial ground for my brethren called Quakers wherin I do appoint my Executor and Trustees to inter my body when deceased. . .'. This land was situated in the northeast corner of what became the garden of the 'The Poplar Inn', Sutton Road. In the late 1990s the inn was demolished in preparation for a housing development. Before building could start, an archaeological excavation took place in order to determine whether any Quaker burials had occurred there. No evidence was found and no burials at Fovant are recorded in the List of Deeds of Meeting Houses and Burial Grounds in the Wiltshire Monthly Meeting of the Society of Friends covering the period 1648-1837.

Mr Jim Attfield of the Dorchester Society of Friends wrote in October 1998:

> . . . there exists in the Dorset Record Office a small bound book containing a record of Quaker burials in Wiltshire listed in order of their sites. The book is undated but must be at least 150 years old. It contains the following entries for Fovant:

Abell James	22. 7.1709;
Wife of James	10.11.1702;
Dunn Elizabeth	26. 3.1708;
Hillard William	22. 7.1702'.

Elizabeth Dunn's place of burial is left blank.

> . . . in the Record Office is a schedule made in 1852 concerning Elizabeth Dunn's orchard which has the following note attached: "The above piece of ground has been for many years lost to the society of friends and cannot now be identified in 1848. J.R. (John Rutter)". . .

That so many of the diehard Quaker family names (Abbott, Day, Strong, Merryweather and Scammell) appear in subsequent Fovant Parish Registers, would seem to suggest that at least some members of these families remained in the village, though the 1783 Bishop's Visitation

Records report that, 'There are no Presbyterians, Anabaptists or Quakers in the Parish, and the Parishioners are decently regular.' However, nonconformity was alive and well in the village, biding its time.

The first sign of that time having arrived for Fovant became apparent in 1815, when a group of local people began meeting for prayer and worship in The Cottage, one of their own houses. Following the practices of a sect known as 'Dissenters', they wished to express their religious beliefs differently from the Established Church.

The establishment of Fovant Chapel.

> Those whose names are mentioned below have assembled together on the 2nd August 1815 at Fovant with one accord and free consent to be affectionately united together in Church fellowship for the purpose of receiving the ordinance and of attending to mutual subjection and church discipline according to the laws of Christ to bear reproof with affection and to give reproof (when requisite) in the spirit of weakness considering themselves lest they also be tempted.
>
> On this solemn occasion an address was delivered by Samuel Hannaford Pastor of the united church of Broad Chalk and Ebbesborne who was also a witness to our union together in the Name of the Father Son and Holy Ghost And may the Lord add unto our number daily such as shall be saved Amen.
>
> Thos Best Junr Teacher
> Ann Scamel Sen
> Ann Scamel Jun.
> Thomas Jay.
> Thomas Scamel.
> Ann Hewlet.'
> Ann Toomer.
> Mary Whatley.
>
> *(extracted from Book 1 of the Chapel Records).*

THE FIRST Chapel baptism, that of Jane Jay, also noted in Book 1, took place on the 28th March 1816. Since this happened before 1820 when the chapel building was opened, the baptism must have taken place in The Cottage.

As membership numbers proliferated, the necessity of acquiring premises suitable to accommodate their growing congregation became patently obvious. They obtained a site in the High Street opposite The

The Chapel interior

Cottage, the venue for their earlier prayer meetings, and began building a new place of worship. With a minimal budget at their disposal and using largely their own labour, the building was completed. An old pocket-book, once in the possession of Mr. John Witt, records that:

> Fovant Chapple was built in the Year of our Lord 1820, by Francis Jay and Wm. Jay his nephew, opened by Revd. Wm. Jay, of Bath, November 22.1820. Text: 48 Psalm.

The Reverend William, born at nearby Tisbury, the only son of a stonemason, initially followed his father's trade. However, after training for the Ministry he concentrated on practical evangelism with such success that he became a national figure in the field. It is tempting to suppose a relationship between the Reverend William Jay, of Bath, who opened the Chapel and Francis and William Jay who built it. Future research may prove a connection, but at the moment we can only conjecture that this was so.

Known at its inception as The Congregational Chapel, its title implies that it followed Congregationalism, an ecclesiastical organisation that left legislative, disciplinary and judicial functions to the individual church and congregation. With such independence firmly in place, the Chapel flourished as membership continued to increase.

The Chapel from the top of the path

Thomas Best, appointed the first Minister of the Chapel in 1815, when it still met in The Cottage, was often assisted by visiting Ministers from nearby Chapels. Whole families, from the eldest to the youngest, started to worship together. Familiar Fovant names, such as Jay, Jarvis, Goodfellow, Strong, Lever, Coombes and Foyle, all feature in the early records of baptisms, weddings or burials that took place there, listed in two old, inexpensive exercise books. Today descendents of some of these families continue to attend services in the

The Chapel Harvest Festival

Chapel. Merged with the United Reformed Church in 1972, it is still known simply as Fovant Chapel and co-exists very amicably with St. George's Church at the other end of the village.

Possibly St. George's Church was not always 'at the other end of the village.' There are rumours that houses on the opposite side of the church to the present village may have been abandoned in the Middle Ages. As the village has developed and grown, it has moved away from the church. The reasons for this are unknown and provide a topic for further research.

The church itself went through some hard times. In 1654 at the Quarter Sessions at 'Newe Sarum' the Minister and Churchwardens presented a plea for help to the Justices of the Peace saying:

> . . . that whereas the parish church of Fovant has for a long time been decaying for want of due and timely repair and is now in our apprehensions in so dangerous a condition that unless the sudden provision be made for the support of it we have just reason to fear least a great part of it may fall down ... some small matters according to the present necessity have been done already in removing the Pulpit and reading seat from a place of danger wherein they stood, to another place more secure. . .

Presumably help was received at some stage, since the building continues to stand securely today. Nowadays the Church Architect makes a thorough inspection every five years and a programme of repairs and maintenance is undertaken to avoid a repetition of the above incident. The responsibility for taking care of the Church was described by one of the current Churchwardens as *'a great privilege but also a great worry'*.

St. George's Church

In earlier centuries, Church attendance on a Sunday was compulsory and the Church was very influential in people's lives. Still to be seen on the outside of the church

Mass dials on the wall of St. George's Church

is a 'Mass Dial', similar to a sundial, which was there to enable the priest to decide the proper time to say Mass. The congregation would, presumably, have been summoned by the bells.

We know that one of the present six bells in the tower is an original from the three which were there in 1553. The newest was presented in 1980 by Miss Hanham, a retired headmistress of the village school, in memory of her mother and brother.

On Wednesday 1st August 2001, a visiting group of bellringers rang a full peal in anticipation of the Queen Mother's 100th birthday on 4th August. This was only the third time a full peal had been rung on these bells, according to the records kept by the Salisbury Diocesan Guild of Ringers and, for the technically inclined, the 5040 changes were rung in 2 hours and 57 minutes.

In today's more secular society congregations are much smaller. The Rector is expected to look after several local churches and hold services in them and the Chapel has visiting preachers. At the beginning of the 20th century congregations were large and attending church was a social event. The following is from *Life and Times of a Wiltshire Farmer* by Bob Combes, whose family farmed the land at East Farm.

Attending Church in 1910

The weekly event that does stick in my mind is the regular visit to Church every Sunday morning, an event I used to dread. The reason for this dread has nothing to do with a distaste for religion - in fact, once I got used to it, I quite enjoyed the sights and sound of the morning service. But to get to Church, we had to walk, Father being too busy to drive us. And at any rate, a walk of a mile and a half in each direction was considered quite normal in those days, even for the legs of a three year old.

So every Sunday morning, we set off at half past ten, up the hill to the main road, then down to the cross roads with a pub on either side of the road, and the village smithy straight ahead. Then a right turn into the village street past the shop and bakery, where sometimes we met the baker. Lucky man, he had to walk only as far as the middle of the village, for he was 'Chapel' and was in fact a lay reader there. I wonder why, when on both sides of the family we had close connections with the Congregational church, we were now adherents of the Church of England? I suppose it was all a matter of position in the village. After all, we might only be tenants, but Father occupied more than a third of the parish acreage and was one of the biggest employers of labour. No doubt Mother felt that, with such a background, it would be unseemly to attend Chapel when by going to Church she would be mixing with the elite of the village. In those days, position was of prior importance, especially when dealing with one's employees and their families.

Further on, past the Church Hall where village entertainments took place, the Fovant Brook followed along the side of the road until it flowed under a little stone bridge to feed the watercress beds. We soon came to the school, nearly there now, with only the Doctor's house to pass, then the Rectory and beyond it was the Church.

Nearing the Church, we met more and more members of the congregation, who exchanged greetings with Mother. Then, just before eleven o'clock, the children arrived from the school, where they had met for Sunday School, under the supervision of the Rector. He, with flowing cassock and books under his arm, shepherded his small reluctant crocodile of a flock towards the Church, with the schoolmistress following as "whipper-in".

Our family pew, inherited from the previous tenants of East Farm, was second from the front on the north side of the aisle, behind that of the Doctor's wife. In all the long years that I was to live in the village I never saw the doctor himself in Church. Not that Father was very much better, but he did come sometimes. When this did happen, our own pew being somewhat abbreviated, the overflow moved into the pew in front. Why we never moved to a larger pew I could never understand, unless to do so would have been to lose face. After all, we could only move backwards, a retrogressive step. The Church choir was not very large, a few boys, one or two elderly men and several young women or girls who were the mainstay of the singing. Mr Blake, the organist, was a truly remarkable character. He had contracted smallpox at a very early age and as a result of that illness had been blind, virtually from birth. He learned to play the organ and the piano and also undertook piano tuning. For more years than I can remember, he came to the village on a Saturday afternoon and stayed the night with friends. He played the organ in

Church at both morning and evening services, returning to his lodgings in Salisbury on the Monday morning.

Any description of the Church in those pre-war days would be incomplete without mention of Mr. Tom (Simper) who was churchwarden. Mr. Tom was a very tall man, with a high, dome shaped bald pate, which seemed to exaggerate his considerable height. In Church he read the lessons and took round the offertory plate and woe betide the member of the congregation who failed to pay up when the plate was shown before him. He would continue to stand before the offender, intoning the words of the offertory hymn in a deep unmelodious voice, until the offertory was duly made. History does not relate that anyone had the nerve to refuse the unspoken but obvious demand.

Enlarging on the story of Mr. Blake, the organist in the description above, a member of a well-known village family commented that his cousin, as a boy, used to pump the organ each Sunday (there being no electricity in the church in those days) and tells the tale that, during the sermon, Mr. Blake would escape outside to smoke his pipe. On his return, if the sermon had not come to an end by the time he felt it should, he would sound a gentle note on the organ. If this did not appear to encourage the Rector to hasten towards the end, a louder note would be played!

The dedication of the Church War Memorial, 1925

Those who still worship at Church or Chapel are well served in the village itself; Catholics will find their nearest church at Tisbury or Wardour and those of different faiths, such as Quakers, must travel further afield – usually to Salisbury.

There are two War Memorials in Fovant, one in the Churchyard and one outside the village hall, near the Chapel. Each November people of all denominations still gather around, while the Rector conducts a service of remembrance and poppy wreaths are laid in memory of those who died as a result of war.

Lowering of the Standards at the annual Drumhead Service

Each summer, for over forty years, Fovant Badges Society has organized a Drumhead Service at the foot of the downs beneath the badges, to commemorate the lives of the people who were stationed here during the First World War and, by extension, all other ex-service people. This is conducted by a visiting clergyman and attended by British Legion members, service personnel, old comrades, local dignitaries and villagers. British Legion and Regimental standards are paraded.

As well as attending services people have different reasons these days for walking or driving along Church Lane; for instance, the cleaning and the arranging of flowers are done by a rota of village volunteers and the churchyard is maintained by a group of volunteer gardeners, who carefully leave the edges of the property in a natural state for the benefit of wildlife. The old Visitors' Book, covering the period from 1978 to 2003, is a valuable social historic document in itself. Who the visitors are, where they come from, their range of ages and why they have visited our church, all make fascinating reading. A good number came to 'find the grave of an old Digger mate' and lament the fact that there are the war graves of so many Australians from 1914–18 who died 'so far from home'.

Some came for practical reasons. Stonemasons and plumbers note the repairs they have made to the fabric of the church and brass-rubbers express their pleasure at the excellence of the memorial brass.

Workmen from the Whitechapel Foundry recorded the removal and re-hanging of the old bells after their re-tuning, together with the hanging of the new sixth bell in 1980. Bell ringers note their visits.

Some came because they, or members of their families, were christened, confirmed or married here and some came to visit family graves or to try to trace ancestors, or just to re-connect with a place where they were happy. 'We have been here for services so often in the past. It's lovely to be back'; 'Fond memories of happy times in the village'

Then there are those who have no particular affiliation to our church but, like so many of us when we are on holiday, have sought out the local church as a place of interest. Many remark on the beauty and peace of the area, or how well the place is cared for. A theme that is constantly repeated is that of gratitude that the church is open, so that the visitor can meditate and pray in such a beautiful setting:

> Lovely peaceful churchyard – dropped in and said a prayer
>
> You are fortunate to have such a beautiful church to worship in
>
> So lovely to find an open church and to be able to take time to pray

It is the comments of such casual visitors, who have no personal emotional association with our church, which underlines the important place that religion still holds in many people's lives.

Of equal importance in this more secular age are visitors who come to research the 'history in stone' that a local church and its surroundings represent: 'Interested in the history'; 'Jethro Crabb – researcher and historian'.

Our old Church Visitors' Book is a historical treasure trove for such visitors. Our current Visitors' Book continues to record not only major events in our villagers' lives, but the comments of all who wish to express their thoughts on visiting our church. Thus is the record kept up for the benefit of all those who come after us.

B.P.

6
Groups and Organisations

GATHERING PEOPLE TOGETHER for the purposes of mutual help, learning or recreation is what builds community spirit. Fovant has been particularly rich in its number and range of groups over time and we are fortunate to have records, photographs and memorabilia for quite a few. These organisations have covered all ages from children to the elderly, have involved both sexes and have included all the social strata of the village.

When looking at the rise and decline of these various groups, it can be seen how they have reflected wider changes in politics and society. The advent of the Welfare State will have meant a reduced need for provident organisations, set up to insure against illness or loss. Greater access to private transport to travel further afield for recreation, as well as the advent of television, will have resulted in less emphasis on village-based sources of entertainment such as amateur dramatics or local sports teams. In contrast, earlier retirement ages and a move towards improved work-life balance will have led to increased demand for group activities to keep both mind and body active.

Benefit Groups

PROBABLY THE EARLIEST groups to be formed in Fovant were those organised for mutual help in times of need. The Fovant Club or Fovant Friendly Society was a sick benefit club which was established in 1767 and ceased in 1911. Its headquarters were in a long, low room on the second floor of the Cross Keys Inn. Club Day was held once a year, always on Ascension Day, and reports of these thoroughly merry affairs appear regularly in nineteenth century editions of the *Salisbury and Winchester Journal*, such as this one dating from 31st May 1851:

> Thursday last being the anniversary of the Fovant old-established Friendly Society, the members met at the clubroom and proceeded to church in an orderly manner, preceded by their honorary members and an excellent band of music, where the Rev. G. Baker delivered an impressive discourse suitable to the occasion, which seemed to rivet the attention of all present; after which

Fovant Club Annual Parade, 1911

> they returned in the same manner, and partook of an excellent dinner, served up by Mr. and Mrs. Ferris at the Cross Keys Inn.
>
> They then paraded the village, calling at the houses of their honorary members (the band playing many national and favourite airs) who in return regaled them with a plentiful supply of cider and good brown stout. The orderly conduct and respectable appearance of the members were very praiseworthy, and the utmost harmony and conviviality prevailed throughout the day.

The Slate Club was also a provident club through which members insured against illness. Charles Turner, a woodman on the estate of the Earl of Pembroke, who kept a diary from 1899–1900, records a meeting of the club on 21st June 1899, although no details are given. The Slate Club was still in existence in 1953 as recorded by Dr. R.C.C. Clay in his description of the village on Coronation Day.

The Fovant Provident Pig Insurance Society, otherwise known as the Pig Club, was set up in 1902 with the object *'to insure against loss the Pigs belonging to the Working Men of Fovant'*. The first President was Sydney Lever and the Secretary was Thomas Wyatt. If any pig insured by means of the Club should fall sick, two members of the Committee would inspect it to ascertain if the illness was due to neglect or ill-treatment. If a pig died, it had to be valued by two Committee members (or the butcher if the members were not available) and the market value was paid to the owner from the funds.

It is interesting to note that Rule 12 stated that 'any member heard swearing or using bad language at any meeting of the Society shall forfeit threepence for each offence...to go to the funds' which seems to be an early version of a 'swear box'. In his diary, Charles Turner recorded that on 19th October 1899 the Fovant Pig Club Supper was held. So, as with the Friendly Society, it can be seen that membership of these organisations brought access to social events as well as practical benefits to individuals.

Practical benefits to the community might also be forthcoming, thanks to the formation of crime prevention organisations, such as the nineteenth century Fovant Association for the Prevention of Crimes. A similar function is performed by the current Neighbourhood Watch scheme, formed of sixteen volunteer co-ordinators who are managed by Parish Councillor Mr. Tony Wells. In its early years the scheme was well resourced by the Salisbury-based leadership, but more recently its incorporation with Tisbury, under

April 2nd. 1908

RULES

OF THE

FOVANT PROVIDENT PIG INSURANCE SOCIETY.

Fovant Provident Pig Insurance Society Rules

management from Wilton, has coincided with reduced availability of information and documentation. The Three Towers community magazine is therefore often used as a means of publicising the aims and activities of the scheme. The co-ordinators' reporting of unfamiliar vehicles and suspicious individuals, either noted by themselves or passed on by villagers, has indeed led to arrests, proving the benefits to the community.

Performing Arts

As described, Fovant's village band actively participated in the annual meetings of the Fovant Friendly Society during the nineteenth century. Unfortunately, according to Dr. Clay's 'Notes on the History of Fovant', documents relating to the band that had been kept in the Church Hall were destroyed when the hall was requisitioned by the Army during the 1939-45 War. However, certificates recording successes in Wessex Brass Band Association competitions survive from 1935, 1937 and 1944.

The instruments used by the band in its later years were purchased at the time of the Jubilee celebrations of King George V. John Foyle, the last turnpike-keeper, was at one time bandmaster, while his brother, the bootmaker, was big drummer. This Drummer Foyle was apparently short and stout with a long black beard and a huge paunch on which he balanced the big drum.

Before the Second World War, Sid Wyatt senior, who ran the newsagent's shop next to what is now Latymer House in the High Street, was the bandmaster. Inevitably, the band's activities were curtailed during the war, but in 1945 the then bandmaster Harry Foyle, son of Drummer Foyle, visited the school and asked if any of the pupils, aged up to fourteen years old, wanted to join the band. About sixteen took up the challenge and after being allocated an instrument and learning the C scale, they were paired up with an adult who played the same instrument to learn from their expertise. In 1948, although he continued to play in the band, Harry Foyle handed over the reins to Reginald Dicker, a Tisbury man of great musical knowledge and experience. Mr Dicker had been a musician in the Household Cavalry and had performed at the pantomimes put on at Buckingham Palace by the then Princesses Elizabeth and Margaret. The band flourished under his leadership and many more certificates were obtained during 1948–51, at competition locations as varied as Chippenham, Poole, Southampton, Wimborne, Wincanton and Larmer Tree at Tollard Royal.

Fovant Band, 1954

The band was in great demand to play at village fêtes, flower shows and other events all around the area, but in the 1960s membership began to dwindle as the era of television dawned. Reginald Dicker had already been asked to take over Shaftesbury Band and so, if either band was asked to perform at an event and had insufficient numbers, members from the other band would be asked to join in. This informal amalgamation became formal in the 1970s and Fovant Band ceased to exist, its instruments being handed to the village school to ensure continued musical learning. However, Shaftesbury Band is still going strong and the grandson of Roy Simper, one of those original schoolboy recruits from 1945, is among its members, making the third generation of performers from one Fovant family.

Roy Simper introducing his son Ian to the tuba, 1958

The band's influence continues through other post-1945 players, including Sid Wyatt junior, who only retired from Shaftesbury Band in May 2002 at the grand old age of 88, after 76 years of loyal service. Another band member, who was recruited after the war from the village school, was Bryan Lee, whose son Colin plays the Last Post from the top of St. George's Church tower and at the war memorial by the Village Hall each Remembrance Day. Colin's first playing of the Last Post was in 1968, when he was aged just twelve, and he has played for the village every year since then.

The village church has also been the home of various teams of bellringers whose make-up, often incorporating several members of the same family, has changed frequently over time. Although regular bellringing was part of village life for many years, like so many other community activities, changes to working and leisure patterns in the 1960s and 1970s saw the bells fall silent owing to an absence of ringers. However, in 1980 Miss Hanham, the retired head teacher of the village school, who lived at Sunnydale on the Church Lane crossroads, decided that she wanted to hear the sound of bells once again. She offered to pay for a new bell to take the complement up to six and this proved to be the impetus for other villagers to rally round and fund the cleaning and re-tuning of the original five bells. This was carried out at a foundry in Whitechapel, where the new bell was also cast, and in the meantime the access to the tower was also made safe. Eighteen volunteers of all ages came forward to learn how to play and were taught at Barford St. Martin, Dinton and Compton Chamberlayne churches. The process involved learning the techniques and changes, but with the bells padded to make them silent, which made it very difficult to judge progress, since the ringers could not hear the results of their efforts.

Removing bells for transport to the Whitechapel Foundry

The tower captain was Roy Simper, whose father had been tower captain some years earlier before the bells were silenced. His team of six was supplemented by an additional two teams, headed respectively by Ted Mahoney and Tony Wells. This meant that the ringing duties could be rotated between them and this system thrived for around nine years until ill health and age reduced the numbers available. Only around half a dozen trained ringers now remain, who are called upon to ring at family services and weddings, while also ringing a muted peal every Remembrance Sunday.

Fovant Arts and Musical Entertainers, much better known as F.A.M.E., was launched at the instigation of Barbara McCoy with the help of interested villagers and evolved out of a tradition of putting on entertainment for the older members of the community during the winter. From the beginning, the group planned to put on regular performances and, as a result, the company ran for nearly a decade and presented the following shows:

Year	Show	Producer
1988	Music and Song	Barbara McCoy
1988	The Magic Carpet	Joan Brooks
1989	All on a Summer's Day	Margaret Elwin
1991	A Little Bit of This and That	Margaret Elwin

FAME: 'All on a Summer's Day'

1992	It's Foolish but it's Fun	Margaret Elwin
1993	Money Makes the World Go Round	Margaret Elwin
1994	That's Entertainment	Margaret Elwin
1995	Bits and Pieces	Margaret Elwin
1996	Music Hall	Joan Brooks
1997	Music Hall	Joan Brooks

The producers would start thinking about a theme for the next show in late summer, then put together the linkages and obtain the music. Weekly rehearsals would start in October, and although the first two shows were put on in December, it was felt that this put too much pressure on members with their other family commitments at this time of year. So the subsequent shows took place in January, which helped provide much-needed entertainment to banish the post-Christmas blues.

Programme for 'All on a Summer's Day'

The productions were limited by the size of the stage in the Village Hall, there being only one entrance. In fact, the space was so limited that the producer had to act as curtain opener and prompter as well. However, these difficulties were nobly overcome by John Turner, who made the portable staging which helped to enlarge the Village Hall for other activities, as well as the scenery which the cast were required to help assemble. F.A.M.E. also improved the stage lighting, as well as adding new drapes and stage curtains.

The society was greatly helped by Alice Jay who supplied the musical accompaniment for most productions, with the wonderful ability to immediately transpose pieces of music into a higher or lower key as required by the singers when asked. Thelma Blakeman assisted when Alice Jay was not available, or tapes were used. Initially the group consisted mainly of enthusiastic and experienced amateurs, but the arrival of RADA-trained Margaret Elwin and professional dancer Jenny Berwyn-Jones introduced skills that raised the standard of both individual and team performances.

Everyone involved was willing to help in any way, including a resident from Sling Orchard whose freezer was used to store the interval ice creams, and the occupants of Oakhanger Barn opposite, whose garage would be used to store all items from the back areas of the Village Hall during performances, space which was needed for changing rooms. In this cramped area, performers changed into their costumes, including wigs and coronets, the notable hand-made contribution of Christine Thompson, assisted by Elsie Thick and other members, who obtained an amazing variety of costumes from many sources.

The society ran drama workshops and set up play reading groups as well as organising theatre outings and performing in other villages. The final show took place in Shaftesbury Arts Centre with two performances in aid of charity. The popularity of the shows meant demand always outnumbered available tickets, even with two evening performances and one matinee. Reluctantly, F.A.M.E. ceased its activities after several members left the area and its younger members moved away to pursue their careers.

Women's Groups

THE FIRST MEETING of Fovant W.I. was held in September 1934 in the British Legion Hut, with Mrs. Edith Biggs of Fovant House as President, and the members first sang 'Jerusalem' in 1936. Sutton Mandeville was included in the name from 1962 as the two villages are closely linked. Monthly meetings were held on the afternoon of the third Wednesday of every month and were intended to be educational, with talks being given on a variety of subjects. The meetings also proved to be an effective means of communication around the village, keeping people informed about matters of local interest before the parish magazine came into being.

The early years were dominated by the Second World War and in 1941 a fruit preservation centre was formed to combine the W.I.'s allocation of sugar with locally collected produce to make 646 pounds of jam. The members knitted for the Forces, salvaged waste paper, distributed milk and cocoa to the boys and girls of the village and marched in the Village Victory parade, in the line up between the Home Guard and the Boy Scouts.

Initially business was an important part of the meeting, but later the gathering became much more informal with speakers giving a

WI's performance of 'The Nuns of Fovant'

demonstration of a craft or delivering a talk on nutrition or the work of Guide Dogs. As well as being a social afternoon, the activities enjoyed by members caused various other separate organisations to form, uniting people with common interests. One of these groups was F.A.M.E., which emerged from W.I's Drama Group which provided the entertainment for the annual Christmas party given for the senior citizens of the village. The W.I. Drama Group also entered competitions, including one in which they performed a play specially written for them called 'The Nuns of Fovant'.

The Annual Summer Show, an event which ended in 1985, was the highlight of the year when the cookery and craft skills of the members were put on display, together with flowers and flower arrangements. Specialist judges were engaged and the entries in the Village Hall attracted wide attention, with the standard being consistently high. The overall winner with the most points in all categories was awarded the Drury Lowe Cup, which was donated by a one-time President of the W.I.

The W.I. also took part in the procession of decorated floats, which preceded the annual village fête, as well as helping with the teas. In more recent years the Cake Stall at the fête has been the W.I.'s responsibility. Another benefit the W.I. brought to the village was the instigation of the

WI Summer Show 1974, Prizegiving

weekly Coffee Morning in the Village Hall, started by members in 1989.

In the 1970s there were sixty-nine members, but numbers started to drop in the 1990s as more women began to go out to work. Despite this local decline, Fovant W.I. received some prominence nationally when member Mrs. Judy Snowdon acted as national vice-chairman for three years from 1991. In 2004, with the membership down to only around ten, the Fovant and Sutton Mandeville Women's Institute was formally disbanded.

An embroidered hassock in St. George's Church shows that the Fovant branch of the Mothers' Union celebrated its centenary in 1976. This group was affiliated to the church and gave the female members of the congregation the opportunity to meet once a month, which was particularly important in a small village. The aim was to provide a means of social interaction for young mothers, who might be struggling with their childcare duties on a day-to-day basis while their husbands were out at work. A further benefit was the passing on of practical skills such as cookery and sewing from older members to younger members.

Diocesan records show that in 1914 the Fovant branch of the Mothers' Union contributed to the Missionary Fund and that in 1931 there were forty-three members. In 1927 branch reports list Fovant and Compton Chamberlayne as separate groups, but by 1934 Fovant alone is recorded. It may therefore be during this period that the two branches were amalgamated, because this was certainly the case by the middle of the 20th century. Meetings were held in the Village Hall and started with prayers, reflecting the group's religious origins. Dr. Clay noted in his account of the history of Fovant that the group marked Coronation Day in 1953 in the following way:

> Another tablecloth of stout white linen, with the signatures of all its members worked in different colours, was made by the Fovant branch of the Mothers' Union.

The Rev. Kenneth Cooper, who became vicar in 1974, later offered the use of the then Rectory, now Old Fovant House on the High Street, as a more welcoming venue. Meetings continued there until Rev. Cooper's retirement

WI Fovant Fête 1969, 'Alice in Wonderland'

ten years later, after which he was succeeded by an incumbent with no family, who moved to a smaller property. Mrs. Freda Norris therefore hosted the meetings in her home until the group finally disbanded in the mid 1990s, following the retirement of its enrolling member and an increase in the age profile of its members, owing to the reduction in the number of churchgoing young mothers in the village.

The Young Wives group came into being on an informal basis in the late 1950s, when various ladies with children at home found themselves regularly meeting at the shop and stopping for a chat. Conversation turned to the opportunity of getting together in the evening to get away from the children and to have time to themselves for socialising. As a result, the group started to meet up once a month on Thursday evenings at the Village Hall. Often it was a rush to get there because of the need to wait for their husbands to get home from work (or in some cases the pub!) to take over looking after the children.

The format of welcoming outside speakers on various subjects of interest and the development of craft skills such as flower arranging, was similar to that of the W.I., and the Young Wives would also have a float in the

Young Wives, Children's Party

procession that preceded the annual fete. Other activities were more family orientated, such as holding dances in the British Legion Hut and an annual Christmas party at which husbands and children joined in the fun. In the summer the group would book a coach to take themselves and their children on an outing to the seaside, always stopping on the way back for fish and chips in Blandford.

The Young Wives effectively 'fizzled out' in around 1970, because the members were getting older and no longer had children keeping them at home, which in many instances resulted in their obtaining jobs and having less time for membership, as well as being less reliant on the social network within the village. Reduced numbers meant that the individual cost of the monthly payment for the hire of the Village Hall increased and, as with so many organisations at that time, interest waned with the advent of television and the increase in car ownership.

However, while in its heyday, one of the highlights of the Young Wives' year was their cricket match against the Youth Club, held either on the field that then existed where Clay's Orchard is now, or at East Farm. This event brought the generations together, with mothers playing against children in a spirit of fun and the connection between these two groups was re-emphasised in the joint reunions that were held at the Emblems restaurant in 1996 and 1999. These gatherings of people, who in some cases had not seen each other for many years, were extremely well attended, demonstrating the warmth of the memories held of this period of intense social activity in the village.

Youth Groups

OVER THE YEARS, groups have been formed not just for the adults of the village, but also for its younger inhabitants. The Scout movement had started in 1907 and the 1st Fovant Scout Troop was formed in 1928 under the leadership of its Scout Master, Mr. A.S. Hamilton Cox, who had moved to Gerrard's Cottage in Sutton Road in 1926. A year later, the Cub pack came into being, with Mrs. Kendall as Akela.

In 1931 Mr. Hamilton Cox resigned as Scout Master, and although it is not known who took over, the troop must have been flourishing, because by then it was known as Fovant and District and was taking both Scouts and Cubs from nearby villages. By 1932 the troop consisted of twenty Scouts and

Ken Kenchington and Brian Burton at Scout camp

fifteen Cubs and was being led by Mr. James Dean A.D.C. The venue for their meetings is not known. As the 1930s continued, numbers started to decline and as a result, the Scout troop was closed in 1936 when Mr. Dean left the area, while records show that the Cubs finally closed in 1942/43.

However, in 1954, at the instigation of the teenaged Brian Burton, who had been a member of the Scout troop in Wilton where he was at school, the troop was revived. By this time there were numerous young lads in the village who tended to gather at the Burtons' house, where Brian would show them the knot-tying skills he had learned. The popularity of these informal gatherings led to the suggestion of re-establishing a Fovant Scout troop. The then vicar, the Rev. Homer Hill, was consulted and supported the idea, and after much searching among eligible adults in the village, Mr. Ken Kenchington was prevailed upon to become Scout Master. With the help of Skipper Nash of the Wilton troop and advice from the Wiltshire branch of the Scouting Association, the troop was formed with nine Scouts, Brian Burton becoming the senior Scout, and Mr. Leyland Assistant Scout Master.

Weekly meetings were held in the Village Hall and the group also held camps, sometimes by the pond at nearby Teffont. By 1955 the troop

Scouts' Church Parade to dedicate new standard, 1955

consisted of twelve Scouts and four Cubs and on March 27th 1955 the new troop's flag was dedicated at St. George's Church with an accompanying parade. The troop thrived initially, but by 1958 numbers were down to just six Scouts and six Cubs, following which the troop was disbanded, although some boys joined the Dinton Troop.

The first incarnation of Fovant Youth Club came about in the late 1940s, organised by Mr. and Mrs. McCrae and meeting on Monday evenings in the British Legion Hut on Tisbury Road. As a result of the McCraes' background in showbusiness, a major emphasis of the club at this time was staging shows and pantomimes, which were performed not only in Fovant, but also in other locations nearby, such as Dinton and Wilton. The club would also go on outings to the seaside, visiting resorts as far away as Brighton and Littlehampton and on the way back would stop off at pubs which had a piano and go in and entertain the customers by performing songs, with the permission of the landlord.

After the McCraes left the village, the Youth Club continued, thanks to the efforts of the Rev. Hill and the members themselves. However, once these early members grew up and became involved in other activities, the club experienced a decline and by 1958 had ceased to exist.

FOVANT YOUTH CLUB

VARIETY CONCERT

15th and 16th APRIL at 7.30 p.m.

On the Quayside

1.	**Opening Chorus and Hornpipe**	Full Chorus :—J. Priddle, M. Simper, S. Bond, B. Bracher, A. Lee, A. Spicer, B. Burton, D. Wyman, P. Grant, T. Lord, P. Tizzard, D. Wyatt
2.	**Four Trivialities**	Soloists :—June Priddle Ivor Smart Mary Simper
3.	**Guest Artist**	
4.	**Sketch :—You're in the Navy Now** ...	B. Burton, D. Wyman, D. Wyatt, T. Lord and P. Tizzard
	Paradise Street	Sung and Danced by the Gentlemen of the Chorus
5.	**Song**	Sheila Price
6.	**Mime :—Pedro the Fisherman**	Soloist :—Desmond Wyman Nina :— Sheila Price Supported by T. Lord, B. Burton, P. Tizzard, P. Grant and the Chorus

INTERVAL

Spring in the Valley

7.	**Opening Chorus**	Full Chorus
8.	**Song**	Desmond Wyman
9.	**Mime :—In the Park**	D. Wyatt, T. Lord, B. Burton, P. Tizzard M. Simper, B. Bracher, A. Spicer, J. Priddle
10.	**Piano Interlude**	Mary Bond
11.	**Paris in the Spring**	Sheila Price and Chorus
12.	**The Dream of Spring**	B. Bracher and T. Lord
13.	**Sketch :—Nature Abhors a Vacuum** ...	B. Burton, T. Johnson, P. Tizzard, P. Grant, Tony Lord and Sheila Price
14.	**Song with Chorus**	Mary Simper
15.	**Sketch:—Viewing the old Homes of England**	T. Lord, P. Grant, A. Lee, M. Simper, S. Bond, A. Spicer
	Gavotte	Brenda Bracher and June Priddle
16.	**Finale**	Full Company

The Queen

Pianist: Mr. Harvey Richards   Lighting: Mr. W. Wright   Producer: Miss E. K. Whatley

Youth Club Variety Concert programme

By the early 1960s the village demographics had changed again and consequently there was enough demand from a new generation of youngsters for the Club to be re-formed. The instigator was Maureen Riggs, who with two friends approached Mr Wally Barrow of Manor Farm, asking for

Youth Club Summer Outing, 1948

his help, since he had previously been involved in the organisation of youth clubs while his own children were young and the family lived in Surrey. The Club moved its meetings to Friday evenings, with an emphasis on organising constructive activities, and initially gathered in the Legion Hut.

However, in 1964 the hut was removed to make way for the development of four new bungalows, and so the search was on for new premises. Thanks to the involvement and generosity of Mr and Mrs Derbe Berry of Compton House, Compton Chamberlayne, the workshop of cabinet maker Mr John Briggs, located in an eighteenth century farm building on the High Street, was purchased. Mr Berry loaned the money required, which was paid back over a period of time through fundraising and grants.

As a result, Fovant Youth Club today is one of the relatively few youth groups in Wiltshire that owns its own land and premises, with a 1970's extension having provided the necessary toilet facilities. In 1999 the sale of a strip of land to the owners of the next-door property, Oakhanger Barn, provided the spur for a major fund-raising programme by the committee. The success of this, along with various grants received, has enabled the building to be renovated and a new fitted kitchen area to be installed. Although the outside of the building looks much as it always has, the interior underwent a major refurbishment in 2000–1 to bring it up to date.

The club is now a registered charity and the trustees of the club are the management committee, all of whom work on a voluntary basis.

Membership of the club is open to all young people between the ages of five and sixteen years and it opens on Friday evenings from 6.00 pm to 8.00 pm, catering for young people from the surrounding villages, as well as those from Fovant itself. The activities provided for the members have also been brought up to date, with requests from children for X-Box game consoles playing exciting fast action games, which are a source of great competition between players as well as testing hand-eye co-ordination. Playstation consoles, with dance mats for 'teach yourself' disco dancing, also teach the children the skills of concentration as well as building confidence.

Despite all this modern technology, traditional pastimes such as table tennis, pool, darts, table football and board games are still much in demand and maybe surprisingly, lots of children still love games that could be regarded as old-fashioned, such as bingo. Loud music is always enjoyed by the youngsters, although not always by the poor adults who are supervising.

The Youth Club is affiliated to Youth Action Wiltshire, who offer special activity nights which are subject to a charge, but which might include

Youth Club, 21st century

Giant Games, mask making, mosaic making, seasonal craft activities, making stencil window pictures and outdoor 'It's A Knockout' competitions. Although many things have changed at the Youth Club over the years, chatting with mates and making new friends is always ongoing, showing that the young people of the village enjoy the organised social interaction available in Fovant as much as the adults do.

Sports Clubs

TEAM SPORTS have always been an excellent way of forging community spirit, since it is not only the players themselves who are involved, but also those who come along to watch and support, or who are involved behind the scenes in some way. Fovant is no exception to this and indeed the Salisbury and Winchester Journal of 31st May 1830 reports that on the day after the Fovant Friendly Society's annual gathering, *'the village rural sports commenced, and were kept up with great spirit terminating in some excellent heats between some Jerusalem ponies of the adjoining villages'.*

Summer in the English countryside inevitably conjures up images of village cricket and there is talk of cricket being played at Fovant as early as 1826, but unfortunately this date cannot be substantiated. Although it is not certain when the Fovant Cricket Club was established, the first thoughts of forming a village team seem to have come about during the mid-1930s. This is described by Bob Combes when writing about his father John, of East Farm:

> Our own village postmaster and one or two other keen cricketers proposed that we should form our own Club, and until we could make our own ground, we should play away games only. We found plenty of opponents only too pleased to entertain us, and surprisingly we managed to win one or two matches, and to hold our own against more established sides, and yearned for the time when we had our own ground, and could entertain our own hosts in return.
>
> We did roll out some level patches in some of our fields where we could do some net practice, until Father, seeing that there was sufficient keenness in the village, made a novel suggestion. Instead of trying to make a cricket square out of ordinary pasture, we should lay down a concrete pitch with coconut matting surface, and he set aside one of our pastures for the use of the Club. We found the matting pitch perfectly true, though a bit hard on the

visiting bowlers when their front feet came down hard on the matting. The outfield also left a lot to be desired, especially if the cows had been grazing the pasture at the time.

Cricket team, 1937-8

After John Combes died in 1940, Bob decided to create a permanent cricket ground for the village and accordingly he arranged for the correct grass seed to be sown for both an outfield and square, on an area immediately adjoining the farmhouse, with his front door opening out towards the pitch. In his book, Bob Combes gives more information about the team's progress and key players:

> For the mainstay of the team we had a retired army colonel, who also happened to be a baronet. His fast medium bowling allied to a high-stepping action was most impressive and earned for him the nickname of "The bounding baronet". There was a neighbouring farmer, who was a sound bat, and who bowled most effective "tweakers". For the rest, we had some regular enthusiastic villagers, and gradually began to collect some good club cricketers from further afield, who enjoyed village cricket on a well-prepared pitch among congenial company. A retired brigadier, who in his time had opened both batting and bowling for the Sappers in their annual match at Lords against the Gunners, was our umpire and general advisor.

The earliest official minutes of the cricket club date from 1954, when it was known as the Fovant Cricket and Tennis Club, although the name changed in 1961 following cessation of the tennis activities. The subsequent owner of East Farm, John Williams, upheld the same cricketing tradition, and was Club Captain during his playing years. John Williams' son Edward now holds the position of Club Captain and Club Patron and the cricket pitch remains in the same stunning and unusual setting, unique surroundings which are enjoyed by all the opposition teams who visit.

A wooden pavilion was constructed by Bob Combes at the site in 1959 and a bar licence was obtained in the same year, meaning that Fovant could entertain its visitors with improved hospitality. Bob described this building as *'small but adequate'*, with ample room for changing, a small veranda for spectators and a very small licensed bar where drinks were served by the village schoolmistress, who christened it 'The Slip Inn'. After forty-three years, this structure was replaced during the winter of 2002-3 with a building which had been a holiday home log cabin since the early 1970s on a site owned by the Forestry Commission in North Yorkshire. Following modernisation of the site, some thirty of these log cabins were decommissioned and the advertisement showing them for sale in the Farmers Weekly was spotted by the cricket club chairman, Howard Smith.

A visit by club stalwarts Ali and Andy Nuttall to the disused airfield near Scarborough where the cabin had been stored, followed by weeks of planning, cajoling and hard work, resulted in its eventual removal to its new home in Wiltshire. Once it had arrived, modifications were carried out to the inside of the building to remove the beds and open up the inside to form two changing rooms. The kitchen area was moved and the waterworks were plumbed in. This marked a huge step forward for the club, since it was the first time the team had had a flushing toilet and a shower.

A variety of different levels of cricket have been played at East Farm, starting with friendly games, which still continue to be played on a Sunday in the right spirit. New teams are introduced regularly and sons follow fathers into the team, such as those of the Boatwright family. In 1985 the club progressed into the Salisbury League and then into the local evening league in 1992. In 1999 it was agreed to come out of the Salisbury League and enter the Dorset League, both for geographical reasons and the need for a change of opposition.

The evening league team finishes in one of the top two positions at the end of most seasons, as well as consistently reaching the cup final. The 2004 season finished with the Saturday team winning promotion to Division One of the Dorset League. The ground was also used for a fancy dress cricket match, which formed part of the village's festivities over the weekend of Queen Elizabeth II's Golden Jubilee in May 2002.

Like so many other Fovant organisations, the Football Club seems to have been formed after the Second World War. Once the male youth of the village reached official working age, they were eligible to join the team. Members continued playing for as long as their age, fitness, level of skill and home commitments allowed. In the early 1950s the main organisers behind Fovant Football Club were Mr. Tom Burton, who was chairman, Mr. Fred James, who owned the shop and the Rev. Homer Hill, who was incumbent at St. George's church from 1951 until 1958.

Football team, date unknown

The team played in the Nadder Valley League, whose matches took place on a Saturday afternoon and they travelled to venues such as Wylye, Tisbury and Hindon for away fixtures. Home games were played at East Farm, thanks once again to the generous spirit of the Combes family. Pitches were provided in three different locations over the years, presumably moving according to the need to rotate crops. Training sessions took place on a Sunday morning, which with hindsight seems surprising given the support of the Rev. Hill, since this timetabling inevitably meant that members were unable to attend church services. The team does not seem to have been very successful, but maybe they were true exponents of the old adage that 'it is not the winning but the taking part that counts.'

In the mid-1960s Mr. Tom Burton had a fleet of lorries which was used to deliver watercress from the local beds to various markets. The seven drivers employed decided to make up a football team called Burton's Sports, whose numbers were incremented by friends and relations of the drivers, so not all the players were Fovant based. This team played in the Sunday league which was more of a 'friendly' environment, playing against pub teams and the like, from 1965–68.

Darts Team

A slightly less physical sporting activity is enjoyed by the Pembroke Arms Darts Team.

Hobbies and Interests

IN MORE RECENT YEARS, various groups have formed in order to allow individuals with particular hobbies or interests to share them, or introduce them to others. Once again, these pursuits provide those taking part with valuable and enjoyable, as well as informative, social interaction.

The Brimclose Fishing Club was started in the late 1960s by Mr Wally Barrow, who had moved to Manor Farm in 1958, and its activities take place on an integrated water system, consisting of a stretch of the River Nadder, three-quarters of a mile of the brook and three lakes. The idea of creating a fishery arose from an assessment of the land and the realisation that the water could be utilised as a commercial project. Construction started on the first two lakes in 1971, but ultimately letting the fishing proved to be financially unproductive; so after Wally retired in 1973 and let the farm, he had time to devote to building up the land into what has become a beautiful environmental area. His thoughts then turned towards starting a fishing club for enjoyment, and having discussed the idea with friends who proved to be interested, the club was duly established. The first committee meeting took place in September 1977 in the rather cramped surroundings of the fishing hut, although the Annual General Meetings took place in more comfort, first at the Barrows' home and later at the Cross Keys Inn.

Membership is limited to twenty-five and the purpose of creating a members' club was not only to allow keen locals to participate in this popular sport and socialise at the same time, but also to contribute to the maintenance of the area. The third lake was created in 1985 and now the lakes are stocked with imported rainbow trout, while the brook houses the indigenous brown trout.

One of the village organisations that emerged from the W.I. is the Poetry Group, which was formed in the late 1990s at the instigation of Dawn Turner and which meets once a month, with different members taking it in turns to host the gathering at their home. A topic will have been agreed upon in advance for each meeting and members use their knowledge and love of poetry in all its forms to find appropriate pieces among their book collections. These pieces are then read out loud, provoking lively discussion among the small group of members, who are welcomed regardless of age or gender.

In a similar manner, the Craft Group was formed in the mid 1990's because of falling membership of the W.I., in the hope of creating a new opportunity for ladies no longer interested in membership of the W.I. to meet up. The group gathers once a month for an afternoon of social chat, while individuals work on their own particular piece of craft work, and it assists with charity items being sent to war-torn countries to help deserving causes such as orphanages and the homeless. It costs nothing to be a member, but each takes it in turn, space permitting, to host an afternoon, with the hostess providing tea and biscuits.

The Fovant Gardening Club was formed in late 1983 at the initiation of Mrs. Pam Fenton and Mrs. Anne Harris, who both had a keen interest in gardening and felt that Fovant needed a forum for non-competitive sharing of gardening knowledge, tips and ideas. They placed a notice in the village Post Office and between them generated a considerable amount of interest, which has been maintained ever since, with the club having grown to a membership of around sixty in 2004. Meetings are held in the evenings, on the first Thursday of each month in the Village Hall, and the first speaker was Mr. Wally Barrow of Manor Farm, who delivered a talk on orchids. Now there are seven speakers a year, often specialist growers, nursery owners or college lecturers, who are invited, for a fee, to address the members on their relevant area of expertise. In addition, there is one annual coach outing, often undertaken in combination with other local gardening clubs, such as the one at Teffont, and a couple of car outings. These trips allow members to visit renowned gardens in Wiltshire and neighbouring counties, whether owned privately, or by bodies such as the Royal Horticultural Society, the National Trust or English Heritage. An annual Christmas party means that the social emphasis is, as ever, strongly maintained.

In 1994 a small group of villagers formed an organisation called the Fovant Amateur Artists, following the success of exhibitions which had been held in the Village Hall by Mrs. Lesley Cox to display her work and that of others in the village. The main focus of the group was to widen the scope of these exhibitions to include talented artists, not only from Fovant, but also from further afield, if these could be attracted, using a variety of local advertising methods. The first exhibition by the group as a whole took place on 22nd March 1995 and exhibits in a wide range of media have always been welcomed.

In 1997, after the death of initiator Lesley Cox, a survey was carried out among supporters of the group to find out whether they wanted it to continue. After 20 returns were made in favour, the organisation formalised

Fovant Art Society exhibition, 2003

its business, appointing committee members, producing accounts and holding annual general meetings. In 2000 the name was changed to Fovant Art Society in order to reflect more accurately its aims and activities.

Initially two exhibitions a year were held. Subsequently this has been reduced to one, but demand has led to this annual event being extended, in 2002, from one to two days, to maximise the opportunity for local people to visit, in order to view and, indeed, purchase the items on display. The introduction of the chance for all visitors to vote for their favourite exhibit makes a tour of the display boards more thought-provoking than it might otherwise be.

The Fovant History Interest Group (F.H.I.G.) was formed in 2000, after Margaret McKenzie placed a notice in the village's Three Towers magazine, asking if there was any other local interest in the village's history. Liz Harden, who had already carried out a large amount of research into the village's history out of personal interest, generated through an Open University degree course, responded. Along with Liz's husband Mike, plus Beryl Paton, Sue Martindale and Audrey Nuttall, the group was formed to continue the research and recording of the village's history. There is now a membership of around a dozen, supplemented by much informal help and support from longstanding residents, many of whom have handed over personal photographs and other memorabilia to be catalogued. Members follow their own interest in a particular area of the village's history and

Fovant History Interest Group exhibition, 2004

report at informal bi-monthly meetings. The amount of information and documentation collated has proved to be of great interest to villagers of all ages, when displayed on a stall manned by volunteers at the annual fête, and subsequently on open days at the Village Hall.

The website set up by the group has attracted responses from all around the world, meaning that not only has F.H.I.G. been able to help many people researching family history, but also that it has opened up a new channel of information to further the group's own endeavours to find out more about the village's past.

Jenny Berwyn-Jones moved to Fovant in 1983, and after talking to other mothers at the school gates, decided to start a dancing school in the village, using her professional surname of Paule on the basis that it would be easier for the children to pronounce. As with so many village organisations, the Village Hall was the venue for lessons in ballet, modern, tap and national dancing, once mirrors and barres had been fitted. There was a considerable amount of crossover between the dancing school and F.A.M.E. as both groups made improvements to the hall for the purposes of performances.

Classes were held on weekdays after school, for all levels and for ages from toddlers upwards, but pupils were not entered for examinations. Instead, attention was focused on putting on shows once a year. Four shows had to be held over two successive weekends in order to ensure that as many admiring relatives and friends as possible could attend. When the village school closed and the Rainbow Centre took over its premises and set up a nursery school, Jenny ran classes there, and every year these pupils would put on a small show at the Village Fête.

Also in the 1980s, owing to the popularity of fitness videos, such as the 'Jane Fonda Workout', Jenny responded to demand by starting keep fit classes for adults and subsequently line dancing was introduced as well. The dancing school officially ceased operating in 1992, because the younger pupils had grown into teenagers with other interests and schoolwork to occupy them. However, adult tap lessons plus a range of keep fit classes, some of which incorporate seated exercise for those with limited mobility, are still well attended in 2004.

For a comparatively small village, Fovant has certainly had, and continues to have, many different organisations and groups. They were formed in order to meet a wide range of identified needs, whether to provide some form of community support, to entertain audiences, to inform and educate, or to keep the body physically fit. Over the years these organisations have been supported both practically and financially by dedicated individuals who have given up their time to administer them. Groups have come and gone according to the demographic make-up of the population and changes in work-life patterns. It is most evident that all those villagers who have taken part, or continue to take part, in the activities arranged by these organisations, have derived much benefit from the social interaction involved. This has made Fovant the vibrant community it is today.

M.K.K.

7
Employment

Agriculture

CENSUS RETURNS of 19th century Fovant show that the majority of men, boys and even some women, described themselves as 'agricultural labourers'. This was hardly surprising, for there were several farms in the area and farm work was the chief means of earning a living in Fovant during this period.

Almost without exception the Fovant farms were of the mixed variety. Not only were different crops grown and harvested, but beef and dairy cattle were kept and sheep, poultry and pigs were reared. There were many and varied tasks to be undertaken: ploughing, sowing, planting, harvesting, haymaking, forestry, thatching, hurdle making, milking, sheep shearing, pig killing – the list is endless. Within all these areas were the various 'specialists', such as shepherds, cattlemen, carters, and each had their underlings. The complexity of the cultivation of the soil, the tending of animals and land management argued the need for a large workforce before the days of mechanisation.

In addition to the major farms, many 19th century Fovant residents had smallholdings where they raised crops and kept animals for their own use. Most cottages had large gardens and some villagers also had the use of fields, orchards and allotments within the parish boundary. Cider making and pig killing were communal activities and there were thriving watercress beds in the centre of the village from the beginning of the 20th century.

Cress loaded into one of Burton's lorries

Ing's and Gerrard's Farms are now private houses. We have one 'new' farm in Dean Lane Farm and Manor, East and West Farms are still in operation. They are all still mixed farms. West Farm, however, also has a prize herd of Blonde d'Aquitaine cattle, some members of which, in order to accustom them to people and noise they might encounter at cattle shows, have in the past been taken for walks through the village.

Fovant Blondes being walked along Tisbury Road. Note the historic Weeping Ash trees which were later cut down

In the mid 19th Century there were riots in nearby villages, as agricultural workers, fearing for their livelihood, broke up farm machinery. Resistance to farm machinery may have delayed its use, but it could not halt progress. Gradually, with the development of the internal combustion

Early combine harvester in operation on East Farm

engine, machine power replaced manpower on the farm and as it did so, some of the former agricultural labourers acquired the skills to use the machines and the position of the agricultural labourer began to change. In the 1891 census, for instance, three men describe themselves as 'traction-engine drivers'. There were also two railway labourers.

Other Trades

ALTHOUGH the first census of England and Wales was taken in 1801, it was not until 1841 that the occupation of the individual was noted on the returns. While it is true that in the earliest returns the largest category was that of agricultural labourer, there was also a tremendous range of skilled tradesmen residing in the village.

A man with a trade had a valuable asset, for he could 'shop around' for the best return on his labours. As communications improved, men with a marketable trade arrived - maltster, miller, cordwainer and wheelwright. Some were journeymen, who would stay for a while and then move on elsewhere. Others, masters of their craft, remained to settle and bring up a family in the village. Many of these craftsmen took live-in apprentices, a practice that has a long history as this extract from the Registers shows:

Tradesman's cart delivering bread in Sutton Road

ANTLY, William Hill, of Fovant; to Adam Hill, wool-stapler of Fovant. £20. 1744.

BUGDEN, Robert, son of Robert of Donhead; to Benjamin Drew, butcher of Fovant Stroud. £5. 1729.

DYER, John, son of Mary, widow of Fovant; to John Jarvis, blacksmith of Fovant Stroude. £10. 1717.

GARRARD, William, son of Thomas of Fovant; to George Bowles, cordwainer of Chilmark. £6. 1722.

HARRISON, John, son of Elizabeth of Fovant; to George Goodfellow, tailor of Fovant. £5. 1724.

LEAN, John; to John Phipps, baker of Fovant. £2. 1756.

LIVELONG, William, son of Thomas, of Compton Chamberlayne; to George Lush, the elder and the younger, cordwainers of Fovant Magna. £8. 1715

PHILPOTT, son of John, of Fovant; to John Pear, worsted-comber of Salisbury. £7. 1715.

STACEY, John; to John Jarvis, blacksmith of Fovant. £10. 1754.

WILLOUGHBY William, son of Charles, deceased; to Robert Still, attorney of Fovant. £30. 1724

(from Wiltshire Apprentices and their Masters, 1710-1760, *ed. Dale, Wilts Record Soc. vol. 17, 1961)*

Although the early census returns showed that the majority of the villagers were agricultural labourers, they also noted many who were engaged in other areas of employment. In 1841, for instance, there were four shopkeepers, a tailor, three dressmakers, a glover, six carpenters, a maltster, several cordwainers and even a police constable. The additional inclusion in this census of such trades as an ostler, a post boy, a wheelwright, two carters, two carriers and four blacksmiths, underlines the important part that the horse played in the lives of the past residents of the village. Apart from this variety of Fovant employment opportunities, the existence of village-based horse-drawn carts and carriers as a means of transportation enabled both goods and people to reach out beyond the village. Other forms of transport, namely the mail and passenger coaches, which passed through daily, and the opening in 1859 of the Salisbury and Yeovil Railway, only two miles distant, also widened the choice of employment for local people. The horse-drawn carters and carriers first proliferated, then eventually declined, as the invention of the combustion engine introduced motorised transport to the area.

Carriers' carts in the yard of the Pembroke Arms

Lever's garage on the A30

Some village tradesmen, looking to the future, moved with the times. For instance, as the tractor superseded the horse, so the blacksmith, having acquired the skills to service the motor car, turned his forge into the village garage. Levers Garage, on the A30, originally opened in 1925 by Witt and Lever but subsequently becoming Lever and King, serviced vehicles, sold petrol and even made bicycles to order. They also ran a regular bus service from Fovant through surrounding villages to Salisbury. Perhaps this was the village bus; initially a Bean bought in 1935, later replaced by a blue and cream Commer. Each in turn was housed in a large shed, now the private garage of Riverside, in the High Street.

Village bus - which of the several?

Motor cars were still a rarity at this time, but the Reverend Maitland Arthur Shorland, Rector of Fovant from 1898-1919, owned one of the first private cars to appear in the village. As the following details, taken from *Early Motor Vehicle Registrations in Wiltshire 1903-14*, edited by Ian Hicks (forthcoming, Wilts Record Soc., vol. 58, 2005), show, he was not the only car owner in Fovant during this period:

AM-1465 4 Aug. 1909 - Rev. Maitland Arthur Shorland, Fovant Rectory, Salisbury. 18/22 Scout, four cylinder, (tonneau side entrance body, green, wheels yellow), van body, painted dark blue, 23 cwt; (private), trade, (public conveyance - 12 June 1914)

AM-3606 10 March 1914 - Rev. M.A.Shorland, Fovant Rectory, near Salisbury. 15.9 hp Scout touring car, four-seater torpedo, lavender, approx 23 cwt; private.

AM-4532 1 Dec 1914 - George Harry Cyril Futcher (farmer and parish clerk, West Farm), Fovant, Salisbury. 20hp Ford, four seater, black; 15cwt (private) trade.

A commercial vehicle was also registered to Fovant at this time:

AM-4383 15 Dec.1914. Macdonald Gibbs and Co., Fovant. 20hp Ford delivery van; black; 14 cwt.

In the 1920s a village taxi, owned and run by John Jarvis, made regular journeys to the local market and was also used at weekends for more leisurely pursuits. Coach hire firms, which came into being during the early 1930s, also catered for the holiday trade by offering trips to the seaside or the zoo. Concurrently, Nadder Valley and the Wilts and Dorset Bus Companies, started to run regular passenger services along the A30 between Salisbury and Shaftesbury. Somewhat later, in 1953, Doctor Clay noted in his

Village coach trip, early 1930s

A Burton lorry on its way to market

account of '*Fovant in Coronation Year*', that, 'there are thirty two private cars, and several vans and lorries, and ten to twelve tractors' in the village. Largely speaking, any Fovant-based motorised vehicle at this time would have been connected to one of the village trades. However, the wider private ownership of cars was hovering on the horizon.

Gradually, as motorised transport provided the link between village and town, the need for village-based skills dwindled and with little exception faded away. The introduction of public transport, coupled with a wider opportunity for people to improve their skills, gave rise not only to a wide range of new trades, but also to the possibility of practising those skills beyond the village, whilst still remaining Fovant residents. As the village 'opened up', the increasing affluence of the villagers, coupled with the wider variety of leisure activities on offer, led to the gradual acquisition of more privately owned vehicles. In a relatively short space of time travel by car, bus, train, steamship and air, for work or play, had become commonplace, whilst the horse was mainly used for leisure.

A fine line separates industry from trade. Perhaps it is fair to say that an industry employs the individual skills of a number of trades in order to manufacture a product. Interpreting that definition rather loosely, there were a few areas of employment in Fovant which might have come within the industrial category.

Fovant Quarry, which was situated on the hill behind the Pembroke Arms, was advertising its wares as early as the late 18th century.

Fovant Quarry, Wilts – 1788

Notice is hereby given to all Noblemen, Gentlemen and others, that there is GREEN STONE always ready for sale at the shortest notice of the very best quality, warranted to stand all weather, at the following reasonable prices.

Parpent Stone... at 9d. per ft. cube
Arch ditto... at 7d. ditto superficial
Ashler ditto... at 6d. ditto ditto
Bedstone ditto... at 6d. ditto ditto
Foundation ditto 18 in width... at 6d. a ft. running measure

And every other sort of Stone on the most reasonable terms. All orders will be attended to and executed with dispatch by
Their most obedient and humble servant
Wm.Macey. 16 June 1788. *(After Clay)*

Ten masons were listed in the 1841 census, mainly members of the Jay family, so there must have been plenty of work for them. The quarry was still a going concern into the 20th century, but it is believed that it was filled in with the rubble from the upgrading of the A.30 road through Fovant that took place in the 1950s. Perhaps our stone cottages are made of material quarried in Fovant.

Henry Simper, who was the Quarry master in 1855, also rented Fovant Wood from the Earl of Pembroke. Many men were employed in the management of the woods. Apart from the felling of the trees and cutting up the trunks into manageable proportions, there were such activities as bark ripping, spar and hurdle making and the actual sawing of the wood into planks. There was a sawpit at the top of Mary Barter Lane, just on the point of its junction with the Dinton Road. Sawing a tree trunk into planks was a two-man operation. The tree trunk would be rolled over the top of the pit. With one man at the bottom of the pit and the other at the top, they operated a large cross cut saw to cut the planks.

(opposite) Quit Rent account to Henry Simper, 1848

Mr Henry Simpson

To the Earl of Pembroke Dr

To one Years Quit Rents for the Manors of Teffont Teffont & Dinton to Mich's 1848 viz

	£ - -	£
Teffont	41.7.1	
Teffont	4:13:11	57. 8. 10
Dinton	14.4.10	
	60.5.10	
Deduct the Ann. Allowance for Collectg	2.17.0	

To the Teffont Woods Acct – One Year from Michs 1847 to Michas 1848.–

	£ s d	£ . –	
To the Amount of the Wood &c sold there		223.14.2½	
Deductions.–			
Bill of Disbursements for cutting down Timber Barking & Shrouding	54.2.0		
Do ... for Highway Poors rates & Tithes	15.3.0½		
Do Sundry Expenses	64.1.5		
Cutting down Timber at Dinton – Shrouding &c	8.17.3	174.2.8½	49.11.6
One Years Wages as Woodman to the 30 July 1849	30.0.0		
Allowance for Wood consumed for the Woodmans own burning	1.19.0		
			107.0.4
Mr Robson receives of the late Mr Trueeddock's Exors for Quit Rents for Dinton Mill £9.9.0 pr the Float 1s 6 Annum (subject for Prop: tax to be deducted on the Mill) which is charged in Mr Simpson's Quit Rent Acct to Mich's 1848		9.4.5	8.5.1
Mr Robson paid for Mr Simpson the Teffont fee farm Rent (one Year) to Mich's 1848		0.19.4	
Balance			£ 98:15.3

20th Oct 49. Settled this Acct with Henry Simpson & have received of him the balance hereof

H S Bennett

Edgar Jay, a Fovant resident and no relation to the masons Jay, told that his father 'Herc' was one of a group of workmen brought over to Fovant at the end of the 19th century by Mr. Hitchings of Broadchalke, to remove the Mill wheel and cut out the first watercress beds. An industry of sorts did develop. Cress was harvested, bunched and sold inside and outside the village until 1977, when operations ceased. Three years later the cress beds were converted into a trout farm, known as Springwater Fisheries. After a change of ownership the business became Millbrook Trout Farm.

Domestic Employment

Before the advent of public transport, it was the destiny of many young people to become servants; those who dealt with the more menial tasks involved in household management. As soon as they reached a suitable age, their parents sought a position for them, preferably in 'good' service. Some houses were large enough to employ outdoor as well as indoor domestic servants. Under these circumstances the boys would work for the gardener, the groom or the coachman and the girls would probably start as scullery maids, hoping to work themselves up the indoor hierarchy into something better.

Although Fovant had no house big enough to require such a large domestic staff, there were a few houses in the village of sufficient size to warrant the employment of several domestic servants. In the1851 census, for instance, the village doctor listed a governess and three domestic servants, while the curate reported three house servants and a nursemaid. All of the larger farms, the local public houses and many of the village tradesmen employed domestic servants in one form or another. Even as late as 1901 there were still twenty-three villagers who stated their occupation as 'domestic servant' on the census returns. Some were residential, but many lived elsewhere in the village and came into work daily. Even though change

Domestic staff at Brookside, early 1920s

Indoor and outdoor staff at Fovant Rectory, 1947

was in the air as the 19th century drew to a close, this situation continued well into the 20th century.

It was World War I, with its need for women to fill the jobs vacated by men serving in the army, plus the lack of those same men in civilian jobs, which provided the main catalyst for change. Additionally, the social change engendered by wartime experiences ensured that few would willingly return to being someone else's servant.

Changes in the Labour Market

ALTHOUGH this part of Wiltshire has long had a connection with the Military, Fovant itself had escaped any direct contact with the Army until the latter part of 1915, when the outskirts of the village became a vast training camp. The advent of the Army into the area had a tremendous impact on the village, not least because the farm workers now had the opportunity to earn a greater wage than that offered by agricultural work. From the contractors who first laid out the camp roads and built the huts, through the digging of wells and the building of a power station to supply electricity, to the eventual demolition of the camps, all needed labourers to carry out the work involved. Inevitably, farm workers forsook their work on the land for the more profitable work associated with the camp.

Military camps demolition squad, early 1920s

Other villagers also made the most of the opportunity to enhance their income. Once the camps were established and the regular flow of troops in and out of the camp started, small shops and tearooms proliferated throughout the village. The National Stores, complete with a visiting photographer, set up in opposition to the village shop. A barber started to ply his trade. Local ladies 'took in' washing. The pubs and many private houses did a lucrative trade in accommodation. Officers stabled their horses on local farms and many of them dealt with their finances at the branch of London, City and Midland Bank that opened in the High Street. Although none of these facilities can be classified as military employment, all made their appearance because of the army presence in the village.

Fovant Military Railway, a single track, was opened by the Army in 1915 to connect the camp to the main line at Dinton, two miles away. Civilians were allowed to use this railway and it may be the case that some civilians also worked on the railway. Any such employees, during the strictly military use of the line, would have been classed as military employees working for the army. Apparently the line was used during the demolition of the camps and was not closed down until 1921, after which the people of Fovant returned to their more usual civilian areas of employment.

The National Stores in the High Street

The London, City and Midland Bank

In August 1919, shortly before the demolition of the camps, the Earl of Pembroke held an auction sale of some of his land and property. This sale included most of the village of Fovant. Those residents who could afford to do so took the opportunity to become owners, not only of the houses they lived in, but also of plots of land in various parts of the village. Hard on the heels of the Pembroke sale, building material from the demolished camp was offered to local buyers at knock-down prices. The conjunction of the two events constituted a bonanza for village builders and associated trades - of which they took full advantage - resulting in a spate of village house building, thus enhancing village-based employment opportunities.

Many of the shops that had plied for trade during the period of military presence in the village closed down once the army had left the area. However, there were other, longer-term shops that served the Fovant residents before and after that period and all would have offered an alternative to working as agricultural labourers or domestics.

Trade directories are useful for informing us about what trades were carried on in the village and by whom. For example, in 1867 Mr. Barrett was a plumber and glazier, William Foyle a tailor and Alexander Turner a shoemaker. By 1907 there was a draper, an insurance agent and a coal merchant. In 1923 a fishmonger was listed. Frank Targett's butcher's shop, originally in Back Street (now Brook Street), subsequently moved to the High

Burton's lorries lined up in the yard of the Pembroke Arms

Norman's general shop in the High Street

Street. Back Street also housed a coal merchant, a cobbler and Tom Burton's haulage business. The village had at least two blacksmiths. Ernest Wyatt's milk depot was at the bottom of Moor Hill. Little Barrow, a private house, was built on the site of Lever's licensed slaughterhouse and carpenter's workshop in the High Street. A cabinetmaker practised his art in what is now the Youth Club. Norman's small general shop was further up the High Street, as was Truckle's sweet shop.

Nearer the top end of the High Street was the General Store which, in sequence, became Sid Wyatt senior's newsagent shop, the Handy Shop and lastly an upholstery business. None of these businesses still exists, but all in their time presented village-based opportunities for employment, as did Cowdry's Grocers and Bakery, which, in the form of our Village Shop, is still going strong. Originally situated at the northern end of the High Street, it was established towards the latter part of the 19th century by Solomon and Rhoda Cowdry. The list below refers to the price of goods at Cowdry's shop in 1870. The last item on the third line from the bottom, reading 'Baking a tart', is also of particular interest. Many of the villagers at that time did all their cooking over an open fire and therefore had no means of baking food, so they took advantage of the service offered by the local baker.

Item	Price	Item	Price	Item	Price
Sugar	4d. per lb.	Lump Sugar	6d. per lb.	Tea	3s.0d. per lb.
Butter	1s.2d. per lb.	Lard	1s.0d. per lb.	Starch	5d. per lb.
Cheese	9d. per lb.	Currants	4½d. per lb.	Coffee	1s.8d. per lb.
Ham	10d. per lb.	Bacon	10d., 8½d. per lb.	Pork	7½d. per lb.
Peas	3d. per qt.	Flour	1s.1d. per gal.	Bread	1s.1d. per gal.
Candles	6d. per lb.	Composite candles (for chapel)	9d. per lb.	Plain Cake	6d
Mustard	2s.0d. per lb.	Potatoes	10s.0d. per sack	Vinegar	5d. per pt.
Plum Cake	1s.3d.	Meat Pie	1s.10d.	Lamp Oil	3½d. per pt.
Snuff	4½d. per oz.	Tobacco	4s.8d. per lb.	Night-lights	6½d. per box
Coal	4s.0d. per cwt.	Soap	9½d. per bar	Baking a Tart (for customers)	½d.
Scrubbing Brush	11½d.	Calico	5½d., 6d., 8½d. per yard	Stockings	6d., 7d., 1s.2d., 1s. 6d, 2s. 8d.
Children's Socks	6d. and 10d.	Scarf	3½d. and 10½d.	Boots	

After Clay

Village Stores, still open for business

The Cowdry's son Ernest and his sister Eliza, eventually took over the business. They moved The Shop to the top end of the High Street, a position in which Fovant Stores still remains.

In 1937 the Air Ministry opened the limestone caves at Chilmark quarry as a bomb storage depot. Thus RAF Chilmark, only two miles distant from Fovant came into being. Although headed by RAF personnel, for whom houses were built in Fovant, the 'Bomb Dump' as some locals called it, was largely staffed by civilians. Until 1995, when the depot was closed down, many Fovant residents, of both sexes, were employed at RAF Chilmark in a bewildering range of trades or clerical positions.

Most Fovant residents today use their cars or public transport to take advantage of the full extent of employment opportunities that commuting makes possible. However, a relatively wide range of village-based employment still remains. We still have a garage, a post office, Fovant Stores and a doctor's surgery with associated pharmacy from the previous era. Additionally, several small businesses have been set up within the village. These include a furniture restorer, a chartered surveyor, a trout farm, an irrigation service, a stonemason, a hairdresser, a nursery school, a landscape gardener and a restaurant. Several farms are still operative, but each of these is either let, or managed with the minimum of manpower and the maximum of mechanisation.

A.M. and J.O.H.

8
Services

Local government

THE EARLIEST FORM of village government was undoubtedly in the hands of the Church. Since Church attendance was virtually total, most people came under its influence and the fear of hell and the hope of heaven were very effective ways of controlling the populace. It must be said, however, that though the church was mainly concerned with its parishioners' mortal souls, it also cared to a large extent for their physical welfare.

The responsibility for such pastoral care lay largely in the hands of the Churchwardens, who, according to the 1601 Act for the Relief of the Poor, were called upon to nominate annually 'four, three or two substantial householders' to join them in becoming Overseers of the Poor. This group was to be responsible for raising, by taxation,

> such competent Sums of Money as they shall think fit . . . towards the necessary Relief of the Lame, Impotent, Old, Blind, and such other among them being Poor, and not able to work.

A task of considerable complexity.

The Fovant Churchwardens' books date from 1795 and it is interesting to note the repetition of the familiar surnames, Martin, Futcher and Simper, many of whom were re-elected annually. In 1833 our Churchwardens decided that a sum of £56, known as the Poors Money, whose provenance was unknown and which had been in the care of a previous Rector, should be lodged in a Savings Bank. A painted notice board, still to be seen in our church, recording this fact, states:

> By the recommendation of the Commissioners of Charities, the sum of FIFTY SIX POUNDS of the Charity Monies of the Parish of Fovant, was deposited in the Savings Bank at Salisbury on the 8th of January 1833 in the names of the Minister, Church Wardens and Overseers, the interest thereof to be distributed Annually amongst the Second Poor, and those most deserving and receiving the least relief from the Parish.
>
> James Futcher
> Churchwarden

Poors Charity notice board

This charity is still in operation today.

Associated with the Poor's Money is an area of downland close to West Farm in Fovant, known as Poor's Land. Under an Inclosure Act of 1786 for inclosing the common lands of a parish, this small piece of ground, measuring 1 acre and 32 perches, was awarded to the poor of the parish of Fovant in lieu of certain rights of common, which they had previously enjoyed. This strip of land was later exchanged for a similar area nearer to Fovant and was to be 'allotted to the poor of the parish, as the minister, churchwardens and overseers think fit' *(Clay)*

After the Norman invasion, the conquerors imposed their own feudal rule throughout the country. All important posts in Church and State passed into Norman hands and castles were built the length and breadth of the land. All played their part in subduing the resentful English and imposing Norman rule. Additionally, in 1085 Norman commissioners travelled all over England making an assessment of the value of assets, the use of the land, the tenants and the status of the resident peasantry. Nothing and nobody escaped notice and all was recorded in what we know today as the Domesday Book. Fovant had a brief mention in this book, which states that:

> The church itself (St.Mary at Wilton) holds Fovant. TRE is paid geld for 10 hides. There is land for seven ploughs. Of this land 5 hides are in demesne, and there are two ploughs and seven coliberts. There are eight villans and seven bordars with five ploughs. There are two mills rendering 17s 6d and eight acres of meadow, pasture 4 furlongs long and one furlong broad, woodland two furlongs long and one firlong broad. It is worth £7 10 shillings.

TRE – 'tempore Regis Edward' – pre conquest, in the time of Edward I.

Geld – land tax, normally on a Hide, the amount of land considered necessary to support one family.

Demesne – land held by the Lord, not by tenants.

Colibert – a freed man, former slave.

Villan – a villager, not a freeman, subject to the Manor Court.

Bordar – a peasant of lower economic status than a villan.

Furlong – a measure of land 40 perches long. A Perch varied between 14 and 18 feet

Render – to give a customary payment usually in kind, sometimes in money.

With the creation of the first Earl of Pembroke in 1551 the village, being Pembroke property, came under the direct jurisdiction of the Pembroke Manorial Courts. The feudal system, well entrenched by centuries of custom, perpetuated by the Earl, still held sway.

A Manorial Survey carried out for the first Earl of Pembroke in 1631–2 consisted largely of the names of the tenants of the manor and the rents they had to pay. Additionally, extensive Manor Court Rolls listed what service, in time or kind, each tenant owed to the Lord of the Manor. Among the many and various Manor Records were those known as 'Custumals'. According to W.G. Hoskins in his book *Local History in England* these

> set out in some detail the customs of the manor which all tenants were obliged to observe under penalty of forfeiting their tenements in serious cases, or some

monetary fine for more trivial breaches. Manorial custom had the force of law on each particular manor, and was enforced in the manor court.

Undoubtedly the people of Fovant were a captive workforce during this period.

Gradually a more socially aware local government evolved. Coming within Salisbury's civic and episcopal area, Fovant benefited at a distance from the more widespread ministrations of these bodies. Of more direct influence on village affairs, however, was when, with the Public Health Act of 1872, Fovant became a constituent of Salisbury and Wilton Rural District Council. Eventually, with the setting up of the Parish Council in 1896, the villagers obtained a direct link with established local government and so finally had a voice in the ordering of their own lives.

William, 1st Earl of Pembroke

The Postal Service

THE EARLIEST Post Offices were usually housed at Inns. The only duties of the Innkeeper-cum-Postmaster were the acceptance and handing over of letters, the exchange of mailbags and the provision of fresh horses for the Post Boys who carried the mail over the major roads of the country before the establishment of the Mail Coach Service in 1784.

The Pembroke Arms, built in the 1790s to serve the increased traffic on the recently turnpiked Lower Road, currently the A30, was probably Fovant's first postal collecting centre. Almost certainly the pub would have serviced the Penny Post, which, according to John Siggers in his book

Wiltshire and its post marks, operated between Fovant and Salisbury in 1838. We do not, as yet, know how long the Pembroke Arms fulfilled this purpose, but it is likely that such a situation remained unchanged until the arrival of the National Uniform Penny Postage in 1840. Such was the increased volume of the mail sent and received by the people of remote villages and hamlets, that the Post Office was obliged to open 'Receiving Houses' in places hitherto cut off from the general postal network. Fovant benefited early from such provision, for 'there was a post office in Fovant, Wiltshire, by 1846 and it came under the district control of Salisbury.' (*Royal Mail Archives)*

Garage House (above), probably Fovant's first Post Office, with detail (right) showing former front door changed for a window. Note blocked-up post box to the right of the door.

The location of our earliest official Post Office is uncertain, but the current garage house, where the outline of the blocked up post box can be seen, was an early venue. It is almost certainly there where, according to the Kelly's Directory of 1855, our Sub-postmaster at the

> Post Office. John Lever (was) receiver. Letters arrive from Salisbury at 10 min. past 6 a.m. & delivered at 7 a.m. & 4 p.m.; dispatched 12 noon, and a quarter to 8 p.m. The nearest money order offices are at Salisbury & Hindon.

There is an implication here that letters were individually delivered, but we have no record, as yet, of a village postman at that time. Thereafter John Lever continued as postmaster until Thomas Lever, probably his son, followed him. Thomas was in post from 1889 until 1903. During this period 'a telegraph office was opened in Fovant in 1897 and in 1898 a Money Order Savings Bank office was (also) opened'. (*Royal Mail Archives)*

Who took over from Thomas Lever is yet to be discovered, but Kelly's gives Mrs. Catherine Parsons Goodfellow in the post in 1907. How long she remained postmistress is not known, but the village-based position was still in existence until 'the post office (in Fovant) closed in 1917 but re-opened in 1920'. (*Royal Mail Archives)*

Civilians and servicemen outside Fovant Camp Post Office

The most likely reason for this closure is that a post office associated with the World War I camps under Fovant Downs had been opened just outside the village. Obviously of major benefit to the thousands of soldiers who passed through the camps, it is known that civilians were also

Charlie Foyle and Charlie Austin, our first named postmen

The High Street Post Office, early 1960s

Fovant Camp postmark

Fovant Telephone Exchange in the High Street, opened in 1932

permitted to use the military Post Office, so the temporary closure of the village Post Office would have made economic sense.

When the village Post Office re-opened, Mr. and Mrs. Charles Austin ran the business from their house at the north end of the High Street. On this house, now a private residence, the blocked-up post box is still clearly visible. Charles was also our first named village postman. According to the British Telecom Archives it was during the Austin tenure, in August 1932, that a telephone exchange was opened in the village.

After Charles Austin's death in 1961 his daughter Betty Harte took over as Postmistress, still at the Austin house in the High Street and George Harte took over his late father in law's position as postman. In 1964 Betty and George Harte had their new house, now containing the current Post

Office, built at the south end of the High Street. Here Betty continued as Postmistress and George remained village postman until 1987 when Val Wells became our post lady. Rob Hall followed Val after her retirement in 2002 and Betty Harte and her younger daughter Jackie continue to run the Post Office.

Water

BEFORE there was any concerted effort to provide the village with piped water, villagers relied on wells, or dipping, either from the stream, or from one of the many springs that are a feature of the village. Such a spring still runs down the side of Springfield in Mill Lane to a brick built 'cistern' close to the stream. This area was known as 'the Dip', so it was almost certainly a source of water for some people.

(above) Cistern at the bottom of the garden of Springfield in Mill Lane; (right) Standpipe in Tisbury Road.

Running through the village, the stream provided a constant supply of water for any resident living close enough to benefit from such a convenient source. One of our older residents remembers how her father, using a yoke and two buckets, dipped water for the house from the stream in Back Street. Additionally, those houses in the High Street which were not adjacent to the stream bank had 'dipping rights', which permitted them to access the stream through land next to the gardens of the houses opposite.

Between 1922 and 1947 standpipes were installed in the village. Where this water came from and how far it stretched throughout the village is a subject for further research. As a child Ann Barnard (née Lee) remembers that although there was 'a water tap against the wall of the Malt House…we pumped water into the kitchen of Southbank during the late1940s'. There was a public pump at the point of the road where Brook Street converges with the A30.

Village pump situated on the road where Back Street joined the A30, 1926

A deep bore hole was sunk in the garden of a cottage at East Farm to provide water for the 1914-18 military camps, but is unlikely to have extended its services beyond that immediate area. However, in 1947-48 Salisbury and Wilton Rural District Council took up the option of purchasing ministry pumping equipment. Whether this was material left behind after the demolition of the Fovant military camps is not known, but it seems highly likely, since the mains water system, which was laid throughout the village in 1948-50, took its water from the borehole at East Farm.

Sewage

Until the mains water came to Fovant the process of sewage disposal fell into three rather primitive methods. Some households had septic tanks, which were emptied by private commercial arrangement, others had earth closets which no doubt had to change their venue at regular intervals; but for the most part the villagers used buckets. Twice a week the 'night soil' cart went through the village, emptying these receptacles and the accepted story is that the accumulated contents were deposited on a field opposite the Emblems Restaurant on the A30. Apparently there was always a bumper crop on that particular field. Eventually, during the late 1950s/early 1960s, a more hygienic drainage and sewage disposal scheme was installed throughout the village.

Electricity

ALTHOUGH electricity was established by the military for the 1914-18 camps, this was terminated when the camps were demolished. According to Wessex Electricity Company the eventual arrival of electricity in the village was a three-stage affair. The first area to benefit, in 1931, was the south of Fovant and the High Street, which at that time included Tisbury Road. The second stage, in the 1950s, covered the Church, Leatler Close and Dinton Road. The last instalment, in the late 1960s, connected Clay's Orchard and Sling Orchard to the grid. Even a cursory reading of the areas mentioned show up notable exceptions to the Company's supposed coverage.

Rubbish Disposal

UNTIL THE MID 1940S the disposal of household rubbish was something of a hit and miss affair. Much was just dumped in the pit of the unused quarry situated behind the Pembroke Arms, but some found its way into the woods, or was buried in a series of holes dug by the individual householder. It was not until after World War II, when the district council instigated the regular collection of household rubbish, that the village benefited from a more acceptable method of rubbish disposal.

Education

THE EARLIEST REFERENCE we have to any form of education in the village lies in an advertisement in the *Salisbury and Winchester Journal* of the 17th December 1781, informing its readers that in Fovant

The Rev. James Evans of Wadham College, Oxford, proposes to take a few young Gentlemen to Board and Educate on the plan of Private Tuition at the Parsonage House, which is exceedingly convenient, and in an eligible situation for his purpose their airing ground being immediately under his inspection. They will be instructed in the Classics, French grammatically, writing and arithmetic with every other useful and polite Literature. Salary £20 per annum. Entrance a guinea and a half.

As his wishes are only for a few, parents and guardians may assure themselves the greater care and attention will be paid to the health, morals and improvement of his pupils.

A Dancing Master (if required) will attend.

N.B. On the premises is an exceedingly good cold bath. The School will open on 21 January 1782

The following notice in the 28th June 1830 edition of the same publication advertised that a similar establishment existed in Fovant for the opposite sex.

Mrs Bidwell's Boarding School for YOUNG LADIES (and gentlemen under eight) will open on Monday, 12 July 1830.

Board and Tuition for 4-10 years of age.	£12.0s.0d. Per ann.
Above 10 years	£16.0s.0d.

N.B. For further particulars apply at the School.

Despite the rigours of the cold baths for the boys, all the children who attended either of these schools received an education suitable for their status within the privileged classes. Since all these pupils seem to have been boarders, it is reasonable to assume that they came from outside the village. Following the same logic, it is highly likely that children from the more wealthy Fovant families, unless they had a resident governess, were sent elsewhere to school. Obviously only a handful of Fovant children enjoyed the luxury of such an education, so what educational provision, if any, was made for the rest of our juvenile population?

Dame schools are reputed to have operated in the village at various times, but we have no evidence to confirm their existence. In the early 19th century the Chantry Chapel at the east end of our church, now the vestry, was being used as a schoolroom.

Whether this room was for a Day school or a Sunday School, what the curriculum was, or who did the teaching is open to conjecture. However,

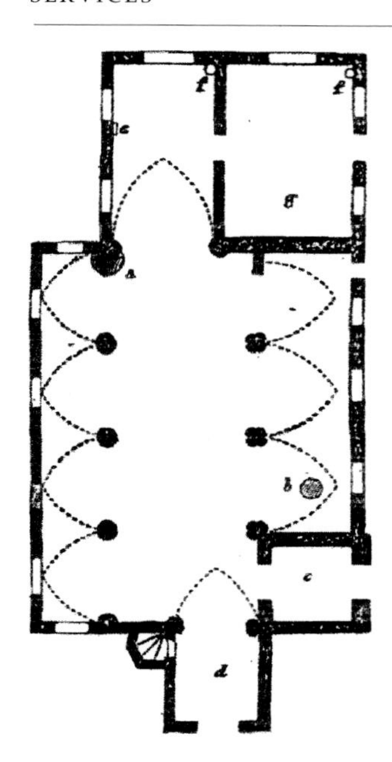

THE CHURCH.

	feet.	inches.		feet.	inches.	
Chancel .	24	6	long;	13	1	wide.
School-room	22	3	long;	15	9	wide.
Nave and Aisles	47	0	long;	27	9	wide.

a Pulpit.
b Font.
c Porch.
d Belfry.
e Brass of Rede.
f Piscina.
g School-room.

Plan of St. George's Church showing the Chantry Chapel schoolroom

Fovant School: sketch made from a lithograph dated 1850

there is no doubt that it is thanks to the Church that the ordinary children of the village got any sort of education at all before our own school was built in the mid 1850s.

The whereabouts of the earliest school logbook is unknown, so information about the school's beginnings can only be an educated guess based on gleanings from other source material. Kelly's Directory for 1885 says that the school was built in 1847 for 150 pupils. The 1841 census lists 141 children between the ages of 4 and 13, but since that particular schedule did not list 'scholars', we have no idea how many of these children attended the school when it opened a few years later. A decade later, in 1851, the census detailed 82 children as 'scholars', but there is no mention of a resident schoolmistress. So who taught these children in the very earliest days of Fovant School and where the teaching staff lived is a mystery still to be solved.

With the 1861 census we have the first mention of a schoolmistress living in the School House. Louisa Good, aged 27, unmarried, born in Devizes, was noted as the schoolmistress in residence. ' A school log book, for this period, states that she was assisted by L.A. Keane, a pupil teacher, and a changing succession of monitors. Other documents accompanying the logbook give us some idea of attendance numbers, subjects taught and the amount of the annual grant assessment.

Fovant School. Grant amounts for year ending 31st December 1866

	Day School	**Evening School**
Average attendance	50 (£10) infants 8 £2.12.0)	19 (£2.7.6)
Presented for exam	48 (£18)	19 (£3.16.8)
Reading	44	17
Writing	41	15
Arithmetic	35	14
Total passes	135	
Total grant	£36.16.2.	
Deductions	£9.12.4.	
Net sum payable	£27.3.10	

(From the earliest school logbook available)

The reason for the deductions was not recorded. The evening school was, presumably, for adults.

Fovant National School

The following summary of a report, after an HMI visit for the purpose of making a grant assessment, is an extract from a letter dated February 2nd 1867, from the Committee of Council on Education, Downing Street, London, to the Rev. E.H. Elers, then Rector of Fovant.

> The children are well behaved and passed fairly in Reading, Writing and Arithmetic; their intelligence however and Religious Knowledge are unsatisfactory. An addition has been made to the grants on account of the scholars who were prevented by epidemic sickness from being present on the day of the inspector's visit. The total grant is however limited by the amount of voluntary contributions and School Pence. (Parental fees – education was not free)
>
> Miss Good's certificate is postponed until My Lords receive a more favourable report upon the intelligence of the scholars and their attainment in Religious Knowledge

Louisa Good's certificate was eventually granted and she stayed in post as headmistress until she married Edwin Lever in the mid 1870s. After her marriage she went to live in Hart's House in the High Street, now called The Firs, leaving the schoolhouse vacant for the next headmistress.

Georgina Fussell, unmarried, aged 22, born in Bradford on Avon, took up this position on 3rd January 1874. Lilian Reade, Bessie Lever, Ellen Coombes, Harriet Thompson, May Hibberd, Annie Keene all feature as Georgina's assistants at varying times during the ensuing twenty two years of her headship. She needed all the help she could get, for payment by results was still very much the order of the day. Every year the children were examined in order to 'pass' in their respective standard. The size of the following year's financial grant depended on how many passes the children achieved.

In loving memory of Georgina E. Fussell, for 22 years Mistress of Fovant National School, who died March 6, 1896, aged 42 years

Georgina Fussell could be said to have given her life to the school, for she died virtually still in post in 1895 at the age of 43 and is buried in our churchyard.

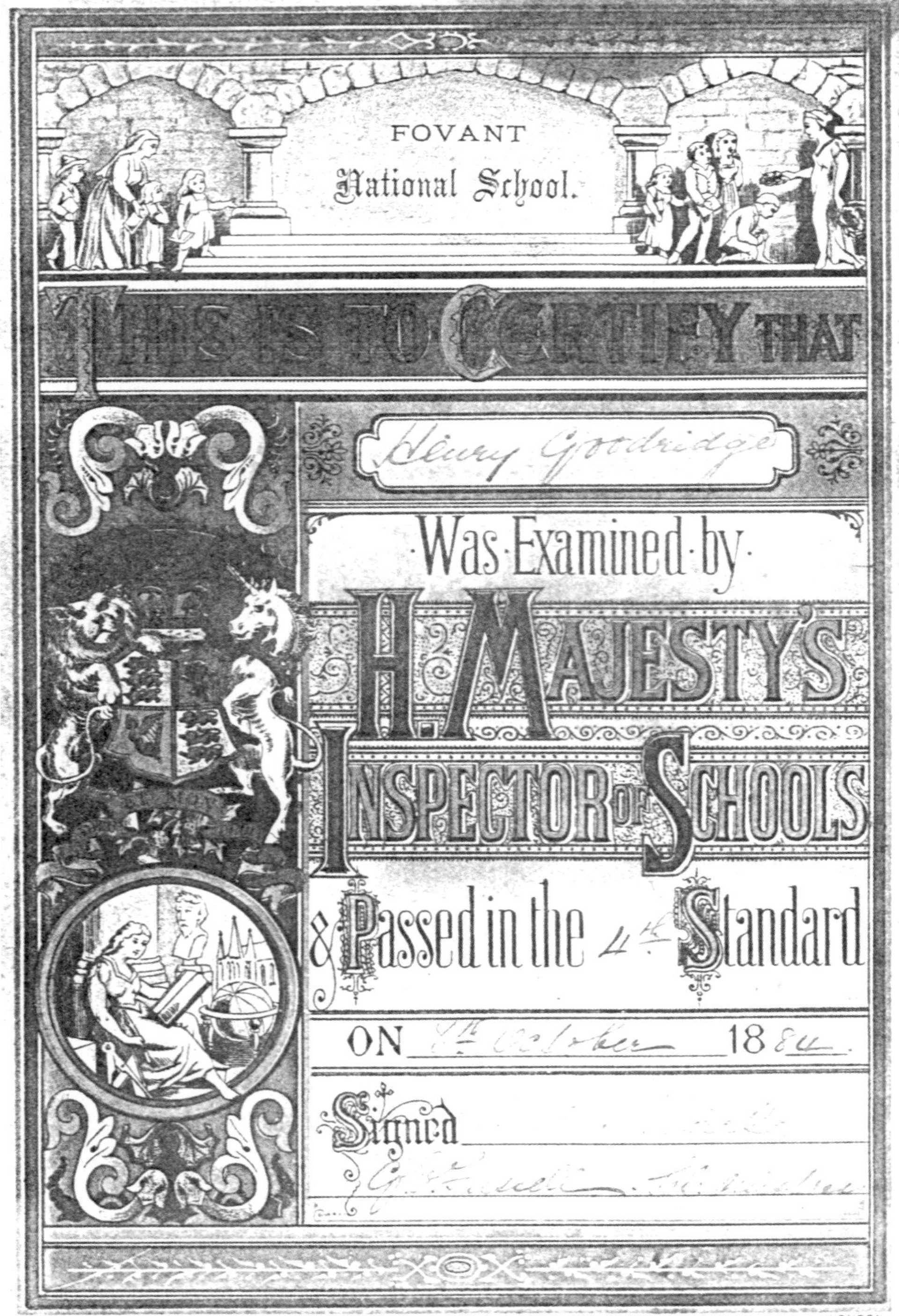
FOVANT
National School.
THIS IS TO CERTIFY THAT
Henry Goodridge
Was Examined by
H. MAJESTY'S
INSPECTOR OF SCHOOLS
& Passed in the 4th Standard
ON 8th October 1884
Signed
ALLMAN
LONDON

Earliest known picture of Fovant School, late 1890s

Edith L. Turner became the headmistress of the school on 23rd March 1896. She and her husband, John, designated a 'paid monitor', became the resident teaching staff of the school. Bessie Lever was still a teaching assistant at this time, but she resigned in 1899. Rose Read, who later became Mrs. Harry Foyle, then joined the teaching staff.

By the beginning of the 20th century the number of children on roll was in the upper nineties, with an average weekly attendance of sixty plus pupils. Their ages ranged from five to fourteen years old. These numbers varied little under the subsequent headship of Edith Pratt and remained relatively stable during the time of Irene Hanham, who followed Edith Pratt as headmistress. However Irene Hanham was still in post when, in response to an aspect of the 1944 Education Act, the twelve- to fifteen-year old children were transferred outside the village for their senior education, leaving only five- to eleven-year old children at the village school.

After Irene Hanham retired in the late 1950s, Doris Bradford took over the headship of the school and she in turn was followed by Henry Scott. It was during Henry Scott's tenure that another change occurred, for in the mid 1980s Fovant came within the Comprehensive education zone. At that stage

(left) Certificate presented to Henry Goodridge in 1884

The last school photograph, Summer 1997

our ten- and eleven-year old children were moved to the middle school in Tisbury.

With yet another reduction in the number of pupils on roll, the long-threatened possibility of closure loomed ever larger. By the summer of 1986, Ian Townsend, who had by then taken over the headship of the school from Henry Scott, was left with only thirty plus children on roll. This number continued to dwindle, eventually descending well beyond the realms of economic viability.

The inevitable closure took place at the end of the summer term in 1997 and our younger children were then assigned to nearby Dinton School, which was considerably enlarged to accommodate them.

(right) Pamphlet advertising the opening of the Rainbow Centre

Our school had been in existence for 150 years. In many ways we were lucky to have had it for so long, for many of the small schools in surrounding villages had long been closed down. The building is now used by The Rainbow Centre which, apart from being used for meetings of various kinds, also houses a privately run nursery school and an after school club for older children.

Medical

THE VILLAGE has been fortunate in having had a resident doctor from the latter part of the 18th century up to and including the present day.

After Fovant's first named medical man Dr Lambert died, a notice in the *Salisbury and Winchester Journal*, dated 2nd May 1763, indicated that Dr Henry Foot of Broadchalke would be taking over the former doctor's house and practice in Fovant. There were several Doctors Foot. Dr. Henry Mitchell Foot of Donhead was the father of Doctor Robert Foot, senior surgeon of Fovant, who died in 1805. Dr. Henry Foot (junior) of Broadchalke and Stephen were sons of Robert. It was Henry of Donhead, the founder of the family, who 'discovered' Foot's Cathartic mixture which, in an undated contemporary advertisement, was reputed to be a cure

For Inflamation in the Bowels.
And Intestines. Indigestion and all
Bilious Complaints.
Discovered more than a Century ago by
Doctor Henry Foot of Donhead St. Mary
In the County of Wilts.
Inflamation in the Bowells and Intestines is
The most painful and dangerous Disease incident
To Mankind, since this Medicine was discovered
Thousands of persons has experienced its most
Happy and Salutary effects many of whom
Were brought to the Brink of the Grave and cast
Off all hopes of Recovery after every other Remedy
Had been tried in Vain and the most Learned
Of the Faculty had been Consulted, this Medicine
Is faithfully prepared from the Original Recipe

FOVANT, DINTON, COMPTON, BARFORD, TEFFONT & BAVERSTOCK

Provident Dispensary and Medical Club.

RULES OF THE CLUB.

The Members shall be all resident within one or the other of the above villages.

The Members shall consist of three classes, First, Second, and Third, and shall pay the rate of the class to which their position in life and income shall entitle them to.

SCALE OF PAYMENTS.

	1st Class.		2nd Class		3rd. Class.	
	Per week.	Per quarter.	Per week.	Per quarter.	Per week.	Per quarter.
Adults above 16 ...	2d.	2/2	1½d.	1/7	1d.	1/1
Man and wife, or wife and 1 child	3½d.	3/9	2½d.	2/8	1½d.	1/7
Man, wife, and 1 child, or wife and 2 children ...	4½d.	4/10	3d.	3/3	2d.	2/2
Man, wife, and 2 children, or wife and 3 children ...	5½d.	5/11	4d.	4/4	2¼d.	2/5
Man, wife, and 3 children, or wife and 4 children ...	6½d.	7/-	4½d.	4/10	2½d.	2/8
A widow and 1 or 2 children	...	...	...	...		1/3
A widow and 3 or 4 children	...	...	...	...		1/9
A widow and 5 or more children	...	...	...	...		2/-

All Subscriptions must be paid within one fortnight from the end of the quarter.

In the event of their not being so paid, a fine of one shilling will have to be paid before re-admission to the club, in addition to usual entrance fee, etc.

All *new* members will have to pay an entrance fee, those in the first class 1/6, those in the second class 1/-, and third class 6d.

Members entering during sickness will have to pay an entrance fee, first class [illegible]s., second class [illegible]s. 15/- 3rd Class 10/ 20/-

Members in arrears with their subscriptions will on no account be attended until their subscriptions and fines be paid.

Members who are able, must attend at the Surgery at Fovant, any day except Sunday, between 9 and 10 o'Clock in the morning, or at the Surgery at Barford between 12 and 1 o'Clock on Fridays.

Members must find their own bottles, &c.

MIDWIFERY.

Members will be attended in their confinements on payment of the following fees :

	£	s.
Those in the 1st class	1	10
" " " 2nd "	1	1
" " " 3rd "	0	15

Half of these fees to be paid at the time of engagement.

Surgeon to the Club,

CHALLONER CLAY, Fovant.

Frederick A. Blake, Printer, Market Place, Salisbury.

By Aaron Ings of Fovant, Grandson of Doctor Robert
Foot and Nephew of the Late Doctor Stephen Foot,
Sold in half pint Bottles at 5s/ each and will keep
Good for 20 years. One Bottle always gives relief
And two or three never fail performing A Cure.

An Aaron Ings features as a young man of twenty-one in the Fovant census of 1841. He is stated to have been of independent means, so he may be the Aaron, great grandson of Henry Mitchell Foot, grandson of Robert Foot and nephew of Stephen and Henry (junior) Foot, who was promoting the 'cathartic mixture'. What is not in doubt is that the Foot family were Fovant's first medical dynasty.

An 1800–55 List of Tradesmen notes four Fovant doctors, John Beckingsale, William Edwards, William Ward and George Wride. From 1855 to 1970 three generations of the Doctors Clay ministered to the medical needs of Fovant and many of the surrounding villages. The Clay family, father, son and grandson, provided the village with its second medical dynasty.

Doctor Robert Richard Clay, reputedly bringing his pack of hounds with him, moved to Fovant in 1855. He took up residence as a tenant of the Earl of Pembroke in the Manor House in Church Lane and established his surgery there. He was followed in the practice by his son, Challoner, who bought the Manor House in the early part of the 20th century. Apart from being the village doctor, Challoner was also surgeon to the Provident and Medical Club, an organisation which, for a 'small' premium, insured against the future cost of medical services.

Richard Challoner Cobbe Clay followed his father and grandfather, taking over the practice in 1917, still at the Manor House. In addition to his patients from the surrounding villages, his list included 120 of the medical beds in the large Military Hospital which catered for the soldier casualties amongst the many men passing through the local military camps during World War I. It is this Doctor Clay, a noted local historian, amateur archaeologist and the author of 'Notes on the History of Fovant', who is pictured overleaf in his consulting room.

(left) Rules of the Provident Dispensary and Medical Club

Dr Clay in his surgery

Since his death in 1971 the village has been well served by four other doctors.

1971	Dr. Legge - at the Manor House
1972-3	Dr. McCauley - at Gerrard's Farm
1974-89	Dr. John Cannon - at Gerrard's Farm
1990	Dr. Gordon Morse, still with us, at Becher's Brook Surgery in the High Street

Although the Midwife and District Nurse Service was mainly based in Fovant, its nurses naturally served a similarly wide area to that covered by the doctors. Lou Winter, of Dinton, recalls Nurse Summerton who nursed her through a severe childhood illness. On Nurse Summerton's marriage she was followed by Nurse Grant. She in turn was followed by Nurse Davies née Frampton, who during WW I met and married an Australian soldier, Dick Davies.

The Davies family settled in the village for many years and Nurse Davies continued to serve the village from 1920 until 1926, when her

Ida Davies, District Nurse 1920-6

Sign for the current surgery in the High Street

increasing family made full-time work impossible. After the Second World War the family emigrated to Western Australia, except for one who chose to stay and who still lives in the village. Many villagers remember Miss Porter, our last resident District Nurse, who initially lived in a wooden bungalow on the area known as the Knap on the Dinton Road, but who moved into one of the Council Houses in Weeping Ash as soon as they were built.

Currently, provision of the services of district nurses, health visitors and all other allied health care professionals is the responsibility of the Local Primary Care Trust. Such people, no longer necessarily village based, drive considerable distances to visit and care for their patients.

Law and Order

Until 1839 the policing of rural Wiltshire was the responsibility of the Parish or Petty Constables, whose ancestors dated from before the establishment of Parliament. Appointed by the Courts Leet, and latterly by the Magistrates in Quarter Session, the constables were supervised by the Magistrates. They were unpaid, untrained and usually unwilling to undertake any protracted investigation. (extract from *The History of Wiltshire Constabulary,* by Paul Sample)

NEVERTHELESS miscreants, once apprehended, were summarily dealt with, as the following report from the *Salisbury and Winchester Journal* shows.

> 17th January, 1757. At the Quarter Sessions of the Peace for the County of Wilts was ordered to be whipt, an old offender Robert Day of Fovant for wood stealing, who we are credibly informed, has been six times committed either to Fisherton Gaol, Devizes or Marlborough Bridewells for different offences in this County only.

Robert Day would appear to have been an 'old lag', but to be whipped for stealing wood is a harsh punishment for a relatively minor offence.

More serious crimes, some of which concerned Fovant people, were not uncommon at this time. As was variously reported in the *Salisbury and Winchester Journal,*

> Robert Futcher of Fovant was set upon by the notorious Bump-Cheek Edwards at Downton Fair (1786)... A horse was stolen from Francis Blundell of Fovant (1788)...the house of William Hayter of Fovant was broken into (1790)...Joel Coombs stole three pecks of wheat from the barn of Thomas Mills at Fovant (1811).

These are just a few of the crimes which were perpetrated in the area, many of which were largely beyond the competence of the Parish and Petty Constables.

In the absence of an effective police force several Wiltshire communities formed private associations similar to this one advertised in the *Salisbury and Winchester Journal* of 15th March 1813.

> Fovant Association for the Prevention of Crimes &c. The Annual meeting of the Association will be holden at the Pembroke Arms Inn, Fovant, on Wednesday next, the 27th inst. The members are requested to attend at 12 o'clock for particular business.
> John Nicholson, Solicitor
> Barford

It is possible that this association emerged from the 'Prevention of Robberies' group, which is mentioned in the August 1792 report of the meeting of the Trustees of the Turnpike under Salisbury Plain, the current A30. This group offered payment of one guinea to informers. How effective such organisations were is open to doubt, but their very existence must have constituted something of a deterrent. However, these moves, which obviously only covered the immediate locality, were symptomatic of the more widespread national situation.

The increasing incidence of crime in the country as a whole had been giving rise to public concern for a considerable period. Pressure for reform intensified as the general populace began to demand protection from such acts of violence. Eventually, after the passing into law of the 1829 Metropolitan Police Bill, the country got its first official police force - in London. Similarly, six years later, after the Municipal Corporations Act of 1835, Salisbury set up its own City Police force. It was not until after the County Police Act of 1839 was accepted by the Wiltshire Court of Quarter Sessions that the small villages of our county benefited from the establishment of a rural police force.

Once the County Police Act became law, action followed swiftly. Captain Samuel Meredith R.N., became the first Chief Constable of Wiltshire when he was confirmed in the post on 28th November 1839. It was a double first, for with this appointment Wiltshire became the first county in the country to have its own Chief Constable.

Meredith was faced with a formidable task. His brief was to

> raise a force of over 200 men, allocate them to areas of patrol, and arrange for their accommodation, supervision, clothing and discipline (and they were to) start their duties from January 1840 onwards. (from *The History of Wiltshire Constabulary* by Paul Sample)

Fovant must have been one of the 'areas of patrol', for in the 1841 census of the village our first resident policeman is listed as: Jas. Mason, aged 30, Police Constable, and his wife Jane also aged 30, Dressmaker, listed as residents, and they were both native-born Fovant villagers.

In each successive census year up until 1901, beyond which details are not yet released, a village policeman is listed as a resident. Being subject to regular 'postings', they rarely stayed very long in any one area.

1851 William Brown, unmarried, aged 23, lodger, born in Sutton Waldron, Dorset.

1861 Martin Jefferies, married, aged 42, born Wooton Bassett, and his wife Mary born Alderbury. No address given.

1864 David White, married to Mary Rosetta, stepson Jephthah, daughter Flora Amanda.

1871 Sidney Carter, unmarried, 28, lodger, born Chitterne.

1881 Sidney Carter, now married, his wife Jane aged 40, born Sherrington, and their two children, both of whom were born in Fovant. No address given. (Unusually Sidney Carter stayed in Fovant for at least ten years.)

1891 Henry King, married, aged 35, born in Castle Eaton, his wife Louisa aged 39, born in Calne, and their nine children, who were born variously at Alvediston, Semley and the last three in Fovant. (A village house, now called Westwood, on the area known as the Knap in Dinton Road, had by now been designated as the Police House. The Kings were the first police family to live in it.)

1901 Alfred J. Perry, aged 29, married, born in Stanton St Bernard, Wiltshire, his wife Sarah aged 29, born in Crewkerne and their children both of whom were born in Fovant. Listed as living on the Knap.

Although further regular records are not yet available to us, Kelly's Directories give Charles Harry Smith as our village policeman in 1915 and an unnamed police constable in 1930. It was undoubtedly sometime during this period that the following incident is likely to have occurred:

> The village policeman saw to it that law and order were respected. The policeman was indeed a law unto himself, administering rough justice to the boys of the village when he caught them in a misdemeanour or minor crime. Physical punishment was never held against him by his victims, so the offender found that any appeal to his parents seldom had any effect. There was an instance when a boy was beaten by a policeman, so Father told me, he complained to his father expecting sympathy. All he got was a second beating, this time by his own father, who said, 'Well, if he thought to beat you, you must have been doing something wrong. So I'll give you a hiding as well, to teach you not to do it again.' Thus was justice doubly served. (from *The Life and Times of a Wiltshire Farmer* by Bob Combes)

The unnamed policeman of 1930 was probably the last of our village policemen to live on the Knap, for in the early 1930s a purpose built police house was constructed. It was situated a little way out of the village on the

P.C. Bond

A.30, in the direction of Salisbury. Apparently, siting a village police house outside a village was a common police practice in order to discourage the policeman from fraternising with the villagers too much. It is doubtful if the policy was very successful.

A succession of village policeman, Police Constables Russell, Bond, Rawlings and finally Martin, then followed each other in the Police House on the A30. Tony Martin was a Traffic Officer rather than an actual village policeman. The local feeling is that the lay-by, which was made fronting the house at a date later than the original construction, was intended for police vehicles. With the building of the new police station at Tisbury in 1974, it was felt that a resident police presence in the village was no longer necessary. Fovant then came under the general jurisdiction of the Tisbury and Mere Constabulary, within which the village became the responsibility of Tisbury-based Community Policemen.

Early in the 1970s the Fovant Police House was sold and became a private residence. Appropriately, the new owners named their house 'Koppergon'.

Although the village has not suffered a great deal from crime in recent years, when a police sergeant in Salisbury asked if local villages would be interested in setting up Neighbourhood Watch schemes, Roy Nuttall volunteered to do so for Fovant. Accordingly, he instigated our group in October 1987. It is still going strong today and reports regularly in our village magazine.

This magazine, although

initiated and launched by the Church, is a Community rather than a Church magazine. Started in July 1989 as a double-sided A4 'News Sheet', it did contain monthly information about church services and celebrations, but it also gave notice of, and reports on, Fovant village events and activities. It quickly outgrew such a minimal reporting space and in March 1990 the organisers announced that

> The present magazine has now been running for a year. In April, Fovant and Sutton will be joining together to produce *Two Towers*. This will be delivered . . . free of charge to all households in both villages'

Thus was born our Community magazine under the joint editorship of Anne Cooke and Sal Margetts, still of A4 size, but comprising a dozen or so pages stapled within an illustrated front cover, which bore the title *Fovant and Sutton Mandeville - Two Towers*, a reference to the respective villages' church towers.

In November 1997, Two Towers became Three Towers, as Compton Chamberlayne was added to the title and the circulation list. The magazine went from strength to strength, supplying news relevant to the community, exchanging opinions and printing small articles considered to be of common interest.

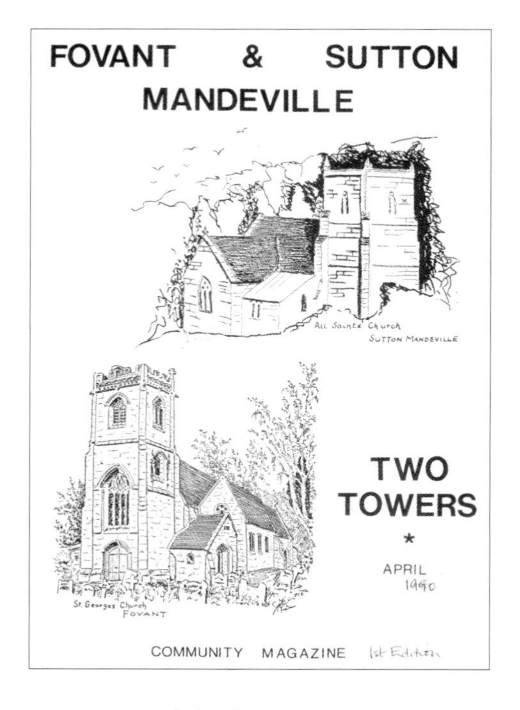

Cover of the first edition of Two Towers, *our Community Magazine*

In the summer of 1999, shortly after the magazine celebrated its 10th anniversary, there was a change of editorship. Anne Cooke deservedly decided to rest on her laurels and, sadly, Sal Margetts died very unexpectedly. In June 1999 Pauline Story took over the editorship and the magazine continues to keep us all in touch with one another.

J.O.H.

9
The Effects of War

FOVANT HAS KNOWN soldiers at least since Saxon times. Its southern boundary follows a byway described in the Saxon Land Charters as Herepath, literally 'Army Path' – a road along which several mounted men could ride abreast.

The village probably witnessed many movements of troops, although no battles are known to have taken place within its boundaries. Perhaps Roman soldiers, certainly Saxons, Danes, Cavaliers, Roundheads and Yeomanry passed this way to nearby battles, sieges and disturbances.

In more recent history, South Wiltshire has been a centre of military activity since the War Office purchased large parts of Salisbury Plain in 1897 to become a training area. Primitive military aircraft flew, and sometimes landed, near Fovant. Military manoeuvres took place on the Fovant Downs as early as August 1898, when the troops celebrated the British victory at

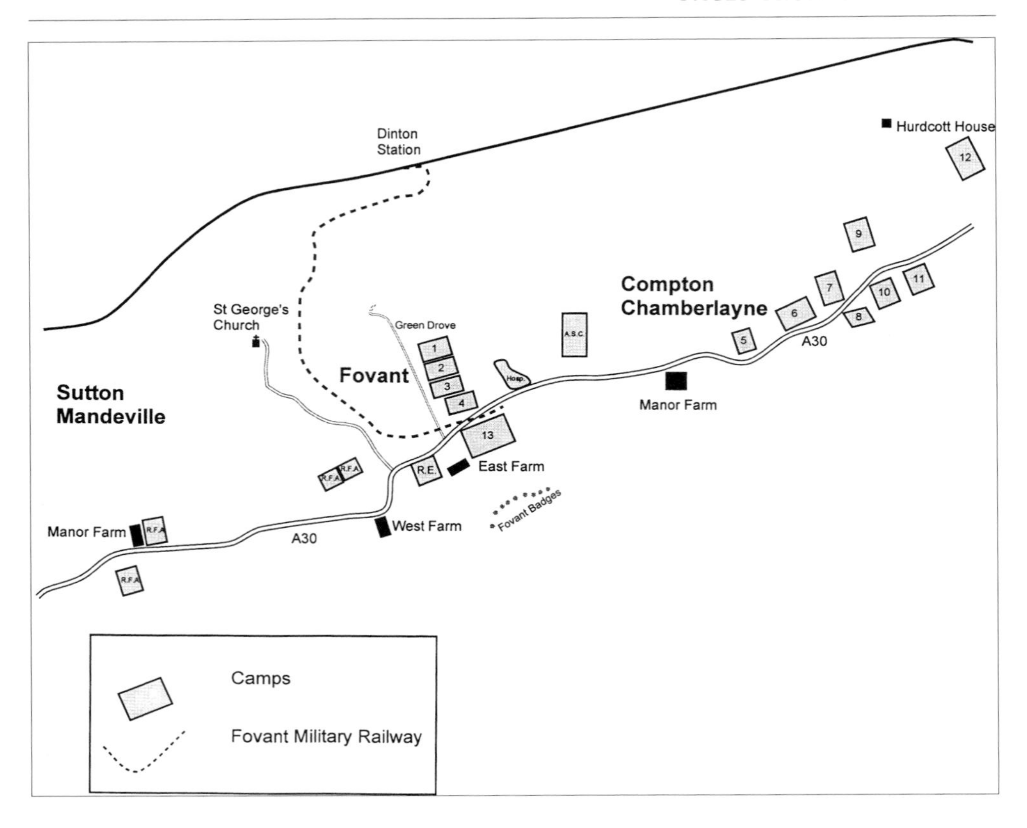

Camps in the area during W W I

Omdurman. Many practice manoeuvres took place in the following years, attended and observed by high-ranking officers of France and Germany. This has given rise to a rumour that the Kaiser visited Fovant in 1909 for one of these exercises.

It was not until the World War of 1914–18 that the village experienced the impact of a great number of soldiers. Large tracts of land were requisitioned from the farmers and the farm labourers found new work with the civilian builders hired to construct the camps, which eventually extended from Barford St Martin to Swallowcliffe.

It is estimated that there were 40,000 soldiers in these camps at any one time. They came from every part of England and from Australia to train or retrain before proceeding to Southampton and on to the various theatres of war.

Iin the lower left corner of the photograph opposite are the East Farm buildings. Beyond the field above them is the A 30, the main road between

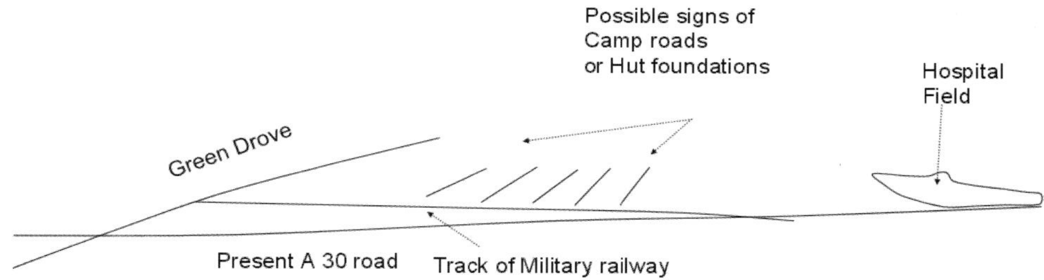

From the Downs in 2003, showing the positions of some of the camps

Salisbury and Shaftesbury, with a row of bungalows on its north side. Fovant village lies behind the trees on the far left, running out of the picture.

A bridleway, Green Drove, runs from the bungalows up to Fir Hill and it is in the large field to the right of this trackway that the squares of the camps can be seen stretching all the way across to Hospital Field, the odd-shaped field on the right surrounded by trees. These camps were known as Nos. 1, 2, 3, and 4, with camp No. 13 in the field south of the A 30, immediately under the downs.

Just south of Hospital Field is the Emblems Restaurant and Beer's Garage and house. It was here that the railway terminal was sited. The track of the railway can be seen quite clearly behind the bungalows and crossing the field at an angle, to intersect the A 30 and end north of the Restaurant and garage. A spur line was built from Dinton station to the camps at Fovant for the easier transportation of supplies, equipment and wounded men returning from active service for rehabilitation and retraining. The troops

Fovant Camp Station

arriving or departing continued to march, often to Salisbury station for entrainment, or up to Salisbury Plain for further training. One of the engines used on this track, named '*Westminster*' was still working in cement works until 1969 when it was sold to a private buyer. After several homes it is now part of the stock on the Northampton and Lamport Line.

Back in 1916 another photographer stood up on Chiselbury Camp. He was an Australian soldier and one of his photographs gives a valuable panoramic view of the whole stretch of camps, and from this panorama the picture opposite has been extracted, so that a comparison can be made with what can be seen today.

After the war, the camps were used as a demobilisation centre. J.R.R. Tolkien was one of many demobbed from Fovant. They were given some money and a rail ticket, except for local boys, who walked home over the downs to Broadchalke and other nearby villages.

There are many picture postcards that not only give an idea of what the countryside and village looked like in that period, but, on the reverse, give a poignant reminder of the feelings of men and women far from home and aware of the dangers which they faced. One wrote what was obviously the second of several

> . . . to get a couple for Tom and three pretty ones for Bena. Don't think I'm

> favouring her pet, I love them all just the same, even our babe though I've only seen him on a photo. I'm hoping something will happen to send me home very soon. They are sending men out very fast now from these camps to fill the gaps and they are hardly marked fit before off they have to trot to France. I'm anxious for Harry as I've not heard. . .

Did he ever get to see his newborn son? So many didn't.

Another shows a view of the High Street and on the back is written

> the place marked with a X is where I take our washing too cheap to do it ourselves. We get a complete change done for 8d so you will see it doesn't pay'

We know that a Mrs Sarah Todd Wyatt (née Jarvis) lived in this house at the time and we know that she took in washing. Her husband was the baker. Parcels of food were gratefully received, even if some of the daintier cakes were rather crumbled by the time they arrived. Socks and pipe were *'just the sort'* one soldier wanted from his mother.

Another tells of the issuing of hot-weather kit, from which they presumed they were bound for the desert of Egypt. A photograph shows them marching off in the pouring rain, splashing through the mud, to eventually board the ship for north France and Belgium. This in December! Others found the camp 'well established with wooden huts and raised roading' and many facilities for recreation.

Photograph from the Downs., showing some of the camps, 1916

More lasting memories of those days are shown in the regimental badges cut into the chalk downs. These, the biggest collection of chalk figures in Europe, make Fovant a tourist attraction. The first to be dug was that of the London Rifle Brigade. There is some discussion concerning how the work was done, but we know that it was willingly undertaken, probably

The Badges, with the rifle range butts below

as a change from the boredom of camp life and training. The soldiers started at 4 a.m. and had to be down again by 7 a.m. when rifle practice began at the targets immediately below the badges. The easiest way down the 30-degree slope was sliding on their shovels!

By the end of World War One there were some twenty badges and many small items such as kangaroos and dingoes; even a Red Cross made with tiles and bricks, as a thank you to the nurses, from some troops leaving for France.

In later years some of these were kept in order by local workers paid by Regimental Associations. The Australian Government make an annual contribution for work on the ACMF badge, the 'Rising Sun' which commemorated the presence of the many Australian troops in the Camps.

During World War Two the badges were allowed to grow over and discolour, so as not to act as a landmark for enemy aircraft. Following the end of the Second World War, the members of the disbanded Fovant Home Guard unit formed themselves into the Home Guard Old Comrades Association. The Association functioned from 1945 until 1960, during which period its members, working in their spare time, not only completely restored many of the regimental badges on the hill, but also cut two new badges of Wiltshire regiments. At its AGM in 1961, it was agreed to change the title of the Association in the hopes of widening its membership. Thus was born the Fovant Badges Society.

Unfortunately, many of the regiments whose crests are carved on the green downland, have disappeared, being amalgamated with others or disbanded altogether. Monetary contributions dried up, so minimal maintenance was undertaken. In 2000 the Badges Society renewed its structure and began the multiple tasks of reviewing the state of the carvings, the work needing to be done on them and the fundraising that would be necessary.

Entertainments, other than that of cutting the Regimental crests, were supplied by various groups. Touring troupes met mixed receptions, but the soldiers' own concerts were riotously received by the troops and the locals alike. Some formed themselves into semi-permanent concert parties and performed in other venues. The Australians' *Kangaroos* were particularly popular and even put on a show in the New Theatre in Salisbury.

Covers of Camp Concert programmes

All sorts of sporting activities filled spare time and probably added to the fitness of the men. The Divisional Cup for soccer was won outright by the East Lancs. and still holds pride of place in the town of Accrington. Many indoor and outdoor activities - tennis, cricket, snooker - were all popular. Some ingenious contests gave much enjoyment to the villagers, who often gathered round to witness greasy pole fights, blind boxing and sack races. They may not have added to the dignity of those who took part, but it gave some light relief from the serious business of rifle and bayonet practice, trench digging and 'square bashing'

A cinema, run by the Navy and Army Canteen Company, showed the latest films. Admission was 3d or 6d, 1/- for a reserved seat - which was probably an essential, as the films were very popular, especially with the children. Bob Combes in *'The Life and Times of a Wiltshire Farmer'* tells how thrilled he was to be introduced to such screen heroes as Charlie Chaplin and Mary Pickford.

Recreation included tennis and cricket

The YMCA was active in the camps, providing quiet rooms for individuals and groups to pray and study or hold services of worship. They set up canteens, which provided writing materials, soft drinks and biscuits and many other comforts for the soldiers. They also arranged concerts for entertainment and, judging by the programmes which have survived, these were rather more decorous than those put on by the Camp Concert Parties. One of the acts was a 'step and clog dancer'. We wonder how this was received? A hut for accommodating visitors who came to see patients in the hospital was provided by the YMCA when it was realised that all the available accommodation in the village was taken.

There was a large hospital in Fovant, shown as Hospital Field on the map, with 21 beds for officers and 588 for other ranks. Hospital huts were, like the rest of the camp, wooden with a corrugated iron roof. A wood stove in the centre gave some heat during the cold wet winters. It was staffed by military nursing staff as well as by local people. Some locals came from nearby villages, but most were from Fovant. Dr R.C.C. Clay, newly installed as local GP, taking over his father's practice, was in charge of 120 medical beds. Milk was supplied by the Langdons of Naishes Farm. Grandson Willie can remember, as a boy of 5, visiting the farm and going with his uncle Joe to deliver the milk to the hospital. The Sister in charge of the ward took him to the kitchens, where he was allowed to hold some newly-born kittens, a memory that has lasted 90 years.

There was another hospital at Hurdcott, manned by Australian Military personnel with the help of locals. It was a Command (Convalescent) Hospital No.3 for patients likely to be fit for duty within 6 months.

At the outbreak of war, the Rev F.E. Hutchinson of Tisbury handed over his vicarage for use as a hospital and this provided 40 beds and was

(above) Royal Army Medical Corps staff (right) Local people who helped staff the wards

Joe Langdon's milk cart

staffed by a Voluntary Aid Detachment, a combination of British Red Cross and St. John's Ambulance personnel. It was included in the Fovant group of hospitals for administration purposes.

A number of regiments of the Australian Imperial Force arrived at the camps in and around Fovant, but the camps at Hurdcott Farm, numbers 5 to 12, were taken over for their use in August 1916. The following March, Hurdcott House became the HQ for No.3 Command Depot of the AIF and within 3 days 1,700 men had arrived from the battlefields of France and Belgium and began settling in. Camps Nos. 5 and 6 were designated as the hospital, but soon that became a secondary hospital with more serious cases being cared for in Camps 7 and 8.

The hospital at Hurdcott had at least 175 beds and probably more. Australian Military personnel - doctors and nurses - staffed it. Some local people worked there and a number of recovering patients helped out as orderlies.

One of these patients was Jack Duffell, who, after being gassed in the trenches, spent 8 months at Fovant until he was declared unfit to return to active duty and was repatriated to Australia. His letters are in the Australian Memorial Museum in Canberra.

Although many of the Aussies found snow a novelty, they were not so enchanted with the rain and mud. One Australian wrote on the back of a photo of the waterfall at West Farm lake,

Australian soldiers enjoying the snow, some for the first time

> They call this a waterfall in England!!? They haven't seen a waterfall over here only what comes from the clouds and that is a good waterfall it is always falling. It never stops. They want to come over to the place they call West. Aust. then they would have something to talk about. What say you Francis . . . from yours Albert, with the best of love.

Another Australian called Fovant Camp

> the largest penal settlement in England . . . country lasses . . . are at a premium and not a few gallant heavy-breathing Anzacs are to be seen walking down the grove after sunset . . . we have a picture show which screens all the latest films up to 1898 AD. Also vaudeville stunts with ladies of the 33rd-class music halls . . . the YMCA library contains a most chaste set of books, General Booth's *Darkest England*, poems by Ellen Wheeler Whitesox

Perhaps he enjoyed the Aussies own Concert party, called the Kangaroos, which performed not only at Hurdcott but also in other camps on Salisbury Plain. The programme for a concert on 15 January 1918 in the Sergeants' Mess had such songs as '*Fritz*', '*the Aviator*' '*Sergeant of the Line*' and '*Homeland*'.

Sports were an important activity, perhaps to keep men fit, but also to overcome boredom. When the camp was disbanded in 1919, items which came up for sale included five pianos, six billiard tables and hundreds of cricket bats.

A special medal for ANZAC Day (April 25th) sports day, held in 1918, was won by Pte Bernard Jack Conlon, serving with the 38th Battalion Australian Imperial Force. He was killed in action in Sept 1918, but his medal is in the Australian War Memorial Museum in Canberra.

Private Conlon's medal

After hostilities had ended, 4 Squadron of the Australian Flying Corps came from the Continent to Hurdcott for demob and smuggled with them, in a haversack, a ten year old French orphan, named Henri Heremene, who had been their mascot for a number of years. A series of photos shows how it was done. They managed to get him back to Australia, where he

Tim and Henri at Hurdcott Camp awaiting transport to Australia

Father and son before Henri joined the Royal Australian Air Force

settled in Queensland with T.W. (Timothy William) Tovell, a mechanic with the 4 Squadron. At 18 years old he joined the RAAF, but, as an alien, could work only as a civilian. When he was 21 he could be naturalised as an Australian and join the Air Force as a pilot, but with only a few weeks to go, he was killed in a motorcycle accident. His grieving adopted family marked his grave with a beautiful headstone showing him as the little boy they had rescued.

Locally there were mixed feelings about this horde of invaders. Some walked out with local girls and a villager still wears the ring given to her aunt by an Australian soldier. Stephen George Jarrett, of the 24th Battalion AIF, played with the Fovant Band, perhaps at a combined concert for the villagers. He was later killed in action near Villers.

An elderly recluse, living on his own in the woods, kept his horse in the kitchen at night 'in case those Australians steal him'.

Fighting on the Continent finished and the AIF came back to Hurdcott for demob. Many months went by and they still could not go home, as shipping was being used for other things. Ill feeling brewed up to boiling point. Bob Combes, of East Farm, tells of his father driving back from Salisbury one evening, being forced to stop by a blockade manned by irate Australians. They would not let him proceed until he had had a drink with them from a barrel they had. He did this quite readily and was allowed to continue to his home.

There were a number who never made it home again. There are 39 Australian War Graves in St George's Churchyard. Gas-damaged lungs could not withstand the ravages of the 'flu epidemic which began in 1918. Many travellers come from 'down under' to see them and one lady even brought a eucalyptus leaf to be laid on each Australian grave.

Military activity in Fovant during the Second World War of 1939–45 was not on the same scale, but nearby U.S.A.A.F. Base Air Depot No 4 brought an American presence into, and often at high speed through, the village. An R.A.F. bomb store had been opened at nearby Chilmark in 1937 and throughout the war the local Home Guard carried out a variety of duties in the area. Both of these organisations were involved when a German Ju88 bomber crashed into Fovant Wood in 1941 and its crew was apprehended, the flight mechanic only after almost a week's search.

When air raids began in earnest on south coast ports, many children were evacuated to quieter villages. Fovant had several and one, Fred

Some of the Australians who did not return home

Harman, has written his memories of his time here. He arrived with his two brothers and was rather apprehensive when a rather fierce-looking woman approached them. She was 'dressed all in black with a hat similar in style to that witches are shown to wear'. But she was willing to take the three of them and was treated with respect by the person organising the placement of the evacuees, so they followed her home. There they were greeted by a younger woman, tall and upright. 'Mother, what are you doing with *three* children?' 'There was no way I was going to see them split up' she replied and Fred realised she was really an angel in disguise. 'Auntie' Annie Hanham and her daughter

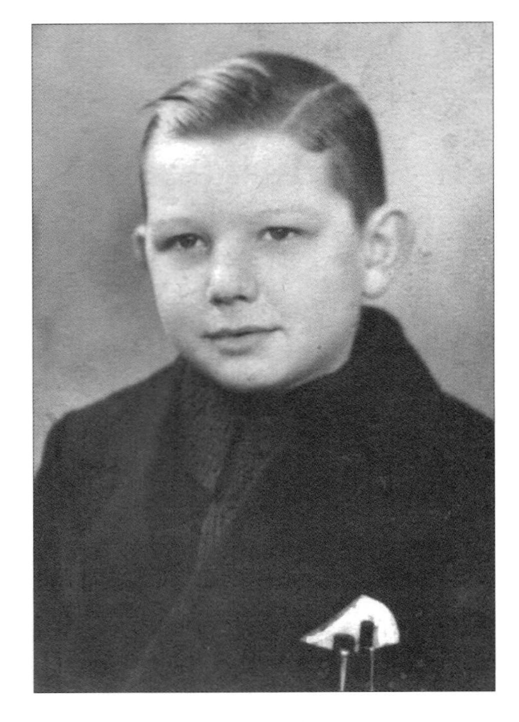

Fred Harman aged 11 in 1938

'Auntie' Rene, the local headmistress, took them in for the duration and became very true and loving friends to the little boys.

Early in the World War Two, Fovant, along with most communities in Britain, set up a group of local men to defend their area in case of invasion. The Local Defence Volunteers became the Home Guard and they met in the lounge of the Pembroke Arms Public House.

We have a constant reminder that warfare brings with it a high cost. In the churchyard are 60 graves of soldiers who died in the hospitals and camps. On the village War Memorial and in St. George's churchyard are named seventeen Fovant men who did not return from that first world conflict. This is a fifth of those who served. The Second World War claimed five men. Many are remembered only as names on the many memorials to the missing in foreign countries. Others lie in named graves from Norway to Italy and from France to Burma.

M.A.M.

Sources used for the Book

Archival and Unpublished *(WSRO = Wiltshire & Swindon Record Office)*
Army Medical Services Museum, Aldershot.
Australian War Memorial Museum, Canberra, Australia.
Bishop's Transcripts and Parish Registers (*WSRO*).
British Red Cross.
British Telecom Archives.
Chapel Records (*WSRO*).
Church Visitors Book.
Dorchester Society of Friends (*Dorset Archives*).
F.A.M.E. Scrapbook.
F.H.I.G. photograph collection.
Fovant Badges Society.
Fovant Church Memorials.
Fovant Enclosure Award and Map, 1785 (*WSRO*).
Fovant family documents.
Fovant Tithe Map and Apportionment, 1840 (*WSRO*).
Fovant Village Plan, late 1970s.
National Census, 1841-1901 (microform in Salisbury Reference Library).
Pembroke Archives - Manor Court Rolls (*WSRO*).
Pembroke Sale Catalogue - August 1919 (*private possession*).
Royal Mail Archives.
Salisbury and South Wiltshire Museum.
Salisbury Diocesan Records (*WSRO*).
Salisbury Reference Library.
School logbooks (*WSRO*).

Printed
Chandler, John (ed.), *Printed Maps of Wiltshire 1787-1844* (Wilts Record Society).
Chatwin, C.P., *The Hampshire Basin* (British Regional Geology).
Clay, R.C.C., *Some Notes on the History of Fovant.*
Combes, Bob, *Life and Times of a Wiltshire Farmer.*
Eicher, Don L., *Geologic Time.*
Geological Survey of England and Wales, *Salisbury* (sheet 298, 1950 ed.).
Hoskins, W.G., *Local History in England.*
Kelly's Directory of Wiltshire, various issues.
Kerridge, Eric (ed), *Surveys of the manors of Philip, earl of Pembroke . . . 1631-2* (Wilts. Record Society).
Ordnance Survey, 25-inch series, 1923 ed.
Salisbury and Winchester Journal.
Sample, Paul, *History of Wiltshire Constabulary.*

Index

NOTE: Fovant places are grouped under the following headings: businesses; farms; fields; houses; inns; roads